THE DESTINY
OF THE DOLLAR

By the same author

The Case Against Floating Exchanges

A Dynamic Theory of Forward Exchange

The Euro-Dollar System: Practice and Theory of
International Interest Rates

The Euro-Bond Market

Foreign Exchange Crises

The History of Foreign Exchange

Leads and Lags: The Main Cause of Devaluation

A Textbook on Foreign Exchange

Decline and Fall? Britain's Crises in the Sixties

The Case Against Joining the Common Market

Parallel Money Markets
(two volumes)

THE DESTINY
OF THE DOLLAR

PAUL EINZIG

MACMILLAN
ST. MARTIN'S PRESS

First published 1972 by
THE MACMILLAN PRESS LTD
London and Basingstoke
Associated companies in New York Toronto
Dublin Melbourne Johannesburg and Madras

Library of Congress catalog card no. 71–18560

SBN 333 13425 7

Printed in Great Britain by
R. AND R. CLARK LTD
Edinburgh

Contents

Preface

THE restoration of the strength of the devalued dollar is of the utmost importance to those of us who want to live and die as free men. For the decline of its strength and prestige before its devaluation undoubtedly reduced the ability of the United States to help to defend our freedom. It is therefore in our own interests to put up uncomplainingly with any unfavourable consequences of any harsh measures adopted or to be adopted by the United States for the sake of restoring her balance of payments.

The adoption of an unexpectedly conciliatory tone by President Nixon in December 1971 at his meeting with President Pompidou and even more at the Washington meeting of the Finance Ministers of the Group of Ten went a long way towards averting a world crisis and restoring the united front of the free countries. His change of attitude, which might well be described as an 'American miracle', made it necessary for me to rewrite a great part of this book at the last minute when it was ready to go to press – a task which I gladly performed.

This does not mean, however, that it was my duty to abstain from criticising the United States for some of the causes responsible for the deterioration of her financial strength, or to abstain from criticising some of the methods chosen by the Washington Administration in its praiseworthy effort to restore American financial strength. But I trust that the opening paragraph of this Preface has made it quite clear that the hard words I feel impelled to speak about American policies and attitudes are spoken in a sincerely friendly spirit.

Much of the criticism this book contains has appeared already over a period of years in my weekly column in *The Commercial and Financial Chronicle* of New York. I think I am justified in claiming that I have told America more unpopular home-truths in the American Press than any other non-American writer, with the possible exception of Alistair Cooke who, though an American citizen, is British-born. We are both inspired in our criticisms by friendly feelings towards the United States, and it is this feeling which impels us to hit hard in our comments when we are convinced. rightly or wrongly, that hard hitting is called for, in the interests of our American friends themselves.

The destiny of the dollar depends on whether the American people are able and willing to discipline themselves sufficiently to restore confidence in their currency. As things are at the time of writing I have doubts whether the extent of its de-valuation will prove to be sufficient to solve its problem. I sincerely hope that events may prove me to have been wrong.

I take this opportunity to express my long-overdue thanks to the Editors of *The Commercial and Financial Chronicle* for giving me full freedom to criticise in their newspaper their country, even though they disagreed with my criticisms on many occasions.

CLIFFORD'S INN   P. E.
LONDON E.C.4
January 1972

CHAPTER ONE

Devaluation of the Dollar

AT long last the United States Government decided in December 1971 to devalue the dollar. This decision was long overdue, having regard to the fact that the dollar had been grossly overvalued and that its overvaluation had been largely responsible for the gigantic balance of payments deficit. By December 1971 it became obvious that the drastic measures announced by Mr Nixon on 15 August, which included the official suspension of the dollar's convertibility into gold, were unable to solve the crisis. In spite of the import surcharge of 10 per cent and other protectionist measures, and notwithstanding the revaluation or appreciation of most other important currencies, the import surplus continued to be abnormally large and the dollar continued to be subject to selling pressure.

The uncertainty of the prospects of the dollar and of other currencies was largely responsible for the aggravation of the world-wide economic recession. Unemployment continued to increase in the United States, in Britain, in Germany and in other countries. It was becoming increasingly obvious that there could be no recovery unless and until the floating exchanges are re-stabilised on the basis of agreed parities. So long as exchange rates were determined by the caprices of the market and by the degree of arbitrary and uncoordinated intervention by the Governments concerned the international economy remained exposed to the dangers of a trade war and a currency war similar to the experience between the two World Wars. In such circumstances there could be no confidence in future prospects.

Fundamental disagreement between the United States on the one hand and the principal countries of the free world on the other made it difficult to come to terms. In numerous aggressive public pronouncements Mr Nixon and Mr Connally demanded that the imbalance between price levels in the United States and in other industrial countries should be eliminated by the unilateral revaluation of the latters' currencies, leaving the dollar unchanged at its old parity of $35 an ounce of gold. The other Governments concerned were, however, equally adamant in insisting on a devaluation of the dollar as part of the general realignment of parities. The deadlock appeared to be complete.

To complicate matters further, the United States also demanded that there should be a fundamental reform of the international monetary system. Evidently the elaboration of a system to take the place of the Bretton Woods Agreement would take much time. Yet a re-stabilisation of currencies and a removal of protectionist measures were matters of great urgency. To defer them until a new plan is elaborated and agreed upon, and until the conflict over the realignment of parities is settled would have prolonged the period of uncertainty and would have exposed the economy of the free world to disastrous crises.

Admittedly no major disaster occurred as a result of four months of floating exchanges. But this was due to the remarkable absence of causes for the eruption of acute crises. There was, however, an ever-present possibility of political, economic or financial developments which might trigger off a foreign exchange crisis that would be liable to become self-aggravating in the absence of any limits set to the fluctuation of exchange rates.

Fortunately there was a distinct change in the American attitude in December. After a series of inconsistent official statements about the Government's attitude towards a dollar devaluation, the meeting between President Nixon and President Pompidou at the Azores resulted in a definite commitment to devalue. What was even more important, there was a striking improvement in the spirit of the relationship between the United States and Europe. As a result it became possible at the Washington meeting of the Finance Ministers of the Group of Ten to elaborate the new set of parities. The realignment was based on a devaluation of the dollar by 18½ per cent, the parity was raised from $35 to $38. At the same time, the United States agreed to the immediate repeal of the surcharge and the other protectionist measures, relying on the other Governments to make adequate trade concessions to her, failing which the legislation providing for the devaluation could not be introduced to Congress.

It became possible to re-stabilise the exchanges without having to wait until an agreement is reached on the basic reform of the monetary system, in the form of a considerable extension of the use of Special Drawing Rights. It was agreed that the official intervention points should be at 2¼ per cent on each side of the new parities, giving a possible range of fluctuations of 4½ per cent instead of the maximum band of 2 per cent fixed at Bretton Woods. When the markets reopened after the conclusion of this agreement foreign exchange business was reasonably orderly, in sharp contrast with the near-chaotic conditions prior to the agreement caused by the uncertainty of parity adjustments.

It was hoped in December 1971 that the immediate problem was solved. Even though there remained a possibility that the United States might not be satisfied with the trade concessions to be offered by Japan and the Western European countries, in which case the whole question might have to be reopened, no such developments were expected in the foreign exchange markets. On the contrary, the suddenly adopted conciliatory attitude of both United States and France gave rise to widespread optimism about the prospects of an atmosphere of give-and-take.

There remained, however, the problem of a basic reform of the monetary system to be solved. There also remained the question whether the measures adopted for the solution of the immediate problem would ensure a recovery of the dollar's strength and would restore the equilibrium of the American balance of payments.

The question of the basic reform will be discussed in detail in Chapters 2, 19 and 20. It will be seen that the proposed extension of the SDR system gives rise to difficult and complicated problems, some of which are bound to be highly controversial. Quite possibly the improved atmosphere created by the solution of the immediate problem might facilitate the task of dealing with the long-range problems in a spirit of mutual understanding. There are indications that Mr Nixon has come to realise that the period when the United States could virtually dictate to the rest of the free world in the sphere of finance is a matter of the past, and that henceforth Japan and Western Europe will have to be treated as being virtually equal partners.

For that reason alone it became necessary to revise the Bretton Woods system which had been created on the basis of the predominant financial strength of the United States. From this point of view the right thing will happen for the wrong reason. Possibly in the absence of the dollar crisis the United States might have insisted on upholding the rules of the International Monetary Fund as they came to be elaborated largely through her one sided power and influence.

It is to be hoped, however, that the pendulum will not swing too much in the opposite direction. For a long time American statesmen refused to admit even to themselves that the dollar had ceased to dominate the free world. The harsh tone in which Mr Nixon, and even more Mr Connally, was addressing the Governments and peoples of the free world during the summer and autumn of 1971 indicated the extent to which they were suffering from an inferiority complex. In public statements, and even more within the four walls of conference rooms, they behaved in an almost intolerably dictatorial manner, precisely because sub-consciously they were aware that they were no longer dictators. The welcome change of tone initiated by Mr Nixon at his meeting with M. Pompidou at the Azores may be interpreted as indicating the advent of a more reasonable spirit.

Conceivably this change of attitude might lead to a wrong reaction among the statesmen of Western Europe and Japan.

They might feel unduly encouraged to make themselves felt and to repay to the Americans what they had to put up with during the period of American predominance. If General de Gaulle were still in charge of France this would undoubtedly happen. But the spirit of the Nixon-Pompidou meeting at the Azores showed that the latter is now capable of adopting a conciliatory tone, always provided that France is treated with the respect that is due to her on the basis of her past history as well as of her restored power. It is to be hoped that, notwithstanding the combined strength of an enlarged and integrated EEC, and in spite of the spectacular increase of Japan's economic power, the relative importance of the United States will be duly realised and recognised by the whole of the free world. After all, the American economy is still by far the strongest, and the free world owes its freedom very largely to America's military power, in spite of the temporary decline of her financial strength. In the words of *The Economist*, 'The Americans can't be replaced'.

One of the main objects of this book is to emphasise the necessity for other free countries to help the United States in the task of restoring her financial strength, even at the cost of some sacrifices on their part. After all, their security is infinitely more important than the rate of increase of their prosperity. In their own interests Western Europe and Japan should be willing to make sacrifices for the sake of ensuring the restoration of the dollar's strength. But the corollary of their willingness to do so should be the realisation by the United States that their trading partners could not reasonably be expected to bear the entire burden of the cost of rehabilitating the dollar. Their sacrifices in the sphere of finance and trade should be matched by an intensification of American efforts to work out their own salvation.

From this point of view the outspoken remarks made by M. Pompidou some weeks after the Franco-American reconciliation at the Azores, to the effect that there could be no useful discussions of monetary reform until the United States has put her house in order, should serve a useful purpose — provided that they are received in the right spirit in America.

There is a strong tendency in the United States to regard the proposed extension of the scope of the SDR system as an infinitely preferable alternative to the self-restraint needed for restoring equilibrium, just as Britain and other countries had considered American financial assistance as a preferable substitute for unpopular measures needed in order to be able to work out their own salvation. It is high time countries of the free world realised that mutual assistance should be employed as a device to be used not as a matter of routine but as a device to fall back upon in the last resort only.

Another object of this book is to warn against the misuse of the new device as a result of the increasing influence of growth-hysteria. It is true, extensive allocation of SDRs could greatly facilitate expansion and the increase in the standard of living – but only at the cost of escalating inflation. An even weightier objection to the misuse of SDRs is that indiscriminate increase of production would make for even more pollution. It is true, it has become fashionable to pay lip-service to the need for safeguarding the environment. But the temptation to step up growth is too strong for most Governments to resist it for mere considerations of keeping down pollution. If instead of pressing for an extension of the SDR scheme the United States were to concentrate on restoring the strength of the dollar through practising self-restraint in consumption and in investment abroad it would go a long way towards safeguarding environment without checking progress.

This is one of the main reasons – if not the main reason – why I attach the utmost importance to restoring the inherent strength of the dollar, not through pursuing the easy way by obtaining large allocations of SDRs – gifts from the IMF in the form of fictitious book entries in their ledgers – but through recovering the virtues to which the American nation owes its greatness. I shall argue in the next chapter against the conception that SDRs should replace gold and dollars as Central Bank reserves. SDRs can serve a very useful purpose for use in emergencies, but they should be used jointly with gold and reserve currencies.

One of the most deplorable results of the currency crises during the last fifteen years or so, affecting as they did mainly the two reserve currencies, was the desire developed by Britain and later by the United States to divest their currencies from the role of reserve currencies. One of the conditions of national greatness is willingness to assume responsibility and risk. Abdication from the onerous but glorious role of countries with reserve currencies was a sad symptom of the debasement of the Anglo-Saxon character. Mankind has greatly benefited by British supremacy during the 19th century and by American supremacy during the 20th century. It would be a thousand pities to relinquish that role, at any rate in the financial sphere, for the sake of avoiding the risks and disadvantages inevitably attached to it, and especially for the sake of having a good time in the short run as a result of prosperity bought at the cost of uninterrupted inflation. What is even worse, there are indications that, largely for financial considerations, the United States is now inclined to follow the British example to relinquish her lead also in the political sphere.

In Chapter 12, I voice a warning that the security of the free world is being jeopardised for the sake of achieving greater prosperity. It is an extremely short-sighted attitude, for should the United States and Britain come to be reduced to satellite states of the Soviet Union they would be exploited by their Communist overlords in the same way as the present satellites are. For this reason among others it would be an unpardonable mistake on the part of Mr Nixon if he persuaded himself that he is justified in trusting the scrap of paper offered by the Kremlin to ensure American disarmament in return for a promise of Russian disarmament. It is undoubtedly very tempting for Mr Nixon to allow himself to be persuaded that it is safe to trust the Soviet Government's promise, since it would enable him to cut military expenditure and to spend more on buying popularity in election year without endangering the stability of the dollar at its devalued level.

For this reason alone, it is to the interests of the countries of the free world to make sacrifices for the sake of strengthening the dollar, so as to mitigate the temptation for Mr Nixon to deceive himself into reducing the military strength of the United States on which the security of the free world depends. Western Europe *must* contribute much more towards the defences of the free world in cash or in kind. Everything reasonable should be done to assist the United States in restoring the equilibrium of her balance of payments.

On her part the United States should do her utmost to regain her self-respect and the respect of the world by making a supreme effort to recover her financial strength. No sacrifice is too heavy if it is necessary to that end. It will be seen in later chapters that excessive domestic consumption and over-ambitious export of capital have largely contributed towards the weakening of the dollar. To that extent the remedy lies in the hands of the American people and its Government.

Unfortunately, the American nation and its leaders show very little inclination to make the necessary sacrifices in the form of self-restraint. The Budgetary deficit for 1971–72 is of the order of $40 billion. In addition to the orgy of public spending, private spending is also encouraged by pursuing a policy of cheap money. This is not the way for the United States to work out her salvation and to safeguard the stability of the dollar, which came once more under a cloud soon after its devaluation. So long as Americans themselves show such lack of willingness to solve their problems no amount of goodwill by other nations could possibly solve them.

CHAPTER TWO

Dollars, Gold or SDRs?

THE suspension of the convertibility of officially held dollar balances into gold meant the end of the monetary system based on dollars. Even though the annual meeting of the International Monetary Fund that took place some six weeks after that momentous event went through the gestures of the established IMF routine, there was no getting away from the fact that there had occurred a fundamental change – that 15 August 1971 marked the end of an era in monetary history. That meeting witnessed the enunciation of a plan for a basic reform, put forward by Mr Barber. The favourable if guarded response to his proposals gave some indication of the outlines of the new monetary system that might eventually replace the system which had been in operation since 1946. The ensuing realignment of parities in December 1971 was the first step in that direction.

The dollar abdicated from its role as international reserve currency, even though it is bound to take years before its abdication could take full effect. Spokesmen of some leading countries – including the United States – expressed themselves also in favour of demonetising gold. In due course Special Drawing Rights – book entries in the ledgers of the IMF – are to assume the role played formerly by gold and later by currencies that had been trusted sufficiently to be able to fulfil that role.

The plan had an almost unanimously favourable reception. It provided a formula under which, it was claimed, it would be easier for Governments to devalue or revalue, so that even the dollar could be devalued by Mr Nixon whenever necessary. Its adoption would open the door for the creation of virtually unlimited amounts of international liquidity – controlled by the Board of Governors of the IMF – so that an elimination of the American balance of payments deficit or a consolidation of the outstanding dollar liabilities would not create a much-dreaded shortage of liquidity. It would enable the United States to consolidate her excessive external dollar liabilities and it would enable Britain to consolidate her excessive external sterling liabilities. All this it was claimed to be possible to achieve with the proverbial stroke of the pen, even though it would take much time and effort before the details of the formula could be elaborated, agreed upon and applied by the Governments concerned.

What objection could be raised to an ingenious scheme which has so many great advantages? It is claimed to be feasible, on the ground that to a very small extent it is already actually in operation. SDRs have been issued by the IMF, and Central Banks hold them as part of their reserves, albeit that they represent a bare fraction of the total reserves consisting of gold, dollars and other convertible currencies in addition to SDRs. It is suggested, and it will no doubt be argued when debating the plan both before and after its establishment, that the differences between the existing system and the one to be created was only one of degree. But if we remember the size of the excessive dollar and sterling reserves which are proposed to be converted gradually into SDRs, we must realise that this difference in degree is of a formidable magnitude, even without allowing for the automatic increase of the total SDRs through the addition of compound interest on it every year, and, above all, from fresh allocations which the IMF is certain to make in generous measure.

To induce Central Banks to accept unsecured SDRs for which neither the IMF nor any Central Bank or Government is legally responsible, and to hold them as part of their reserves, when the grand total in existence is merely $9·5 billion, is one thing. To be willing to hold them in settlement of surpluses when the outstanding total reaches ten or twenty times that amount, purely on the assumption that they in turn would never have any difficulty in passing them on to other Central Banks, is quite a different thing. Yet, having regard to the inconvenience and potential dangers of a continued 'interregnum' in the international monetary sphere, it was very difficult to object to the plan on the ground that it involves grave risk. After all, SDRs was to fill a vacant throne which had to be filled. But we have to take the risk with our eyes wide open.

One of our objects is to describe the course of events leading to the development of a situation in which there is the maximum of inducement to take such a risk. A generation ago anyone advocating a plan such as the one put forward by Mr Barber on 28 September 1971 would have been regarded as a currency crank. It is bolder than the Keynes Plan that was rejected by the United States Government, which now seems keen enough on the proposed revolutionary reform. Has the mentality of politicians, bankers, economists and Government officials undergone a fundamental change? Or has the situation changed to such extent that the taking of the risk involved has become the smaller of two alternative evils?

Gold was accepted under the gold standard, and is still accepted in unlimited amounts because of its intrinsic value. Dollars were accepted under the dollar standard in unlimited amounts partly because of the undertaking given by the United States to convert official holdings into gold at a fixed parity and partly because of the confidence felt in the ability of the immensely strong and dynamic American economy to redeem the dollar holdings in the course of time by exporting goods and services in sufficient quantities.

But what is it that is expected to make SDRs universally and unconditionally acceptable in ever-increasing amounts by a large number of countries in settlement of their balance of payments surpluses? So long as their total is a small fraction of Central Bank reserves this question presents no problem. If, however, the outstanding amount should run into tens of billions the answer to the above question must necessarily be a matter of great importance.

The IMF is under no obligation whatsoever to convert SDRs either into gold or into currencies 'convertible in fact'. After the original system was established as a result of a decision by the Board of Governors of the IMF in 1967, the final details of its application came to be based on a highly involved formula determining the circumstances in which the IMF is entitled, and even obliged, to instruct a participating Central Bank to convert SDRs held by another participating Central Bank into convertible currencies. As far as is known there has been up to now no hitch in the actual operation of the system on a modest scale.

But its operation depends entirely on the willingness of participants to carry out the obligations they have undertaken. These obligations are not binding, for there is nothing to prevent any participant from deciding to withdraw from the system and thereafter refuse to accept any SDRs without breaking any rule. Indeed it can even claim the re-conversion of the amount of SDRs it had already converted. And even if the rules should be tightened to reinforce the acceptability of SDRs, it must be remembered that some fundamental rules of the IMF were dishonoured with impunity in the past, so that their observance could not be relied upon implicitly.

In 1970 France devalued the franc without consulting the IMF to an extent well in excess of the 10 per cent of its original parities prescribed as the limit of devaluations without consent. And in 1971 Mr Nixon announced the decision of the United States Government, without any preliminary consultation with the IMF, to suspend the convertibility of officially held dollars. These two instances should suffice to show that it would be possible for any Government to contract out of the SDR system at a moment's notice even if the rules concerning withdrawal were tightened.

It seems, therefore, that the security provided by SDRs is far from being ideal. If several important members should contract out it might in given circumstances become impossible for the IMF to induce the remaining members to assume the responsibility for SDRs relinquished by other members.

It may well be asked, why it is that the suggestion to replace
the dollar by SDRs as the reserve currency met with a favourable initial response. Partly because the United States had
already abandoned the role which the dollar fulfilled between
1946 and 1971, so that the SDR proposal arrived on the scene at
a moment when the world was in a receptive mood towards
new ideas in the international monetary sphere. But also
because, largely but not entirely as a result of ill-advised
policies on the part of the American authorities, the dollar of
1971 was only a shadow of the dollar of 1946. Its technical
strength deteriorated during the '50s and the '60s. Its super-
abundance reduced its scarcity value. And the growing
reluctance and declining ability of the United States authorities
to carry out their undertaking relating to convertibility made
Central Banks increasingly reluctant to continue to pile up
unwanted dollar reserves. They continued to do so nevertheless
until 15 August 1971, and in many instances even after. But the
policies pursued by the United States Government made it
increasingly evident that the dollar was no longer suitable to
play the part of reserve currency.

It also became evident that no other Government would be
willing to agree that its currency should assume the role
relinquished by the dollar, even if their currencies were strong
enough to inspire confidence. Tentative suggestions to replace
the dollar by a composite monetary unit to be created by the
countries of the European Economic Community were quite
obviously premature, because the integration of those countries
would have to proceed much further before such a unit could
become qualified for serving the role of reserve currency.

Central Banks have become used to holding a reserve
currency they distrust. Even after the suspension of the dollar's
convertibility they had to buy large amounts to prevent or
moderate an unwanted appreciation of their own currencies. In
the past they were in a position to convert their reserve currency
into gold or to shift their reserves into another currency if
they preferred it. So the idea of accepting SDRs, the convertibility of which would depend on the willingness of at least

the majority of Central Banks to continue to participate in the system and to abide by its rules, did not appear to them unacceptable.

But the main reason why the plan was welcomed must have been the inflationary mentality from which hardly any Government has remained immune. The issue of SDRs would provide yet another device with which to finance growth and which would enable them to take the line of least resistance to inflationary political pressures. It would provide a device enabling them to inflate without paying the immediate penalty in the form of problems raised by a balance of payments deficit. If this assumption should prove to be correct, the new system would be doomed to self-destruction through a misuse of its facilities.

One of the main objects of this book is to argue against the application of the device on an excessive scale. There is much to be said for the allocation of SDRs at a moderate rate as a means for making the supply of reserve currencies more adaptable to reasonable requirements. But there is everything to be said against their issue on a gigantic scale. The way to keep down their issue would be to retain the reserve currency role of any currency that commands confidence, and to increase the amount of monetary gold by raising its price. Suggestions to demonetise gold are fashionable but the idea of replacing it by 'paper-gold' is absurd. The only hope for a permanent adoption of SDRs is to keep down their amount, at least until a prolonged period of their use could come to inspire sufficient confidence in their acceptability to enable the IMF to increase the allocations as and when required.

To enable the IMF to avoid over-issuing, which would discredit the system and would bring about its collapse, it would be necessary to rehabilitate the dollar and even sterling so that they should command the necessary degree of respect to qualify them to serve as reserve currency. Other currencies, too, should be eligible, provided they are sound. The allocation of SDRs should not be an alternative to the adoption and maintenance of sound policies. The United States and Britain should not feel that, thanks to this new device, they now could and should allow their policies to be influenced by growth-hysteria. SDRs could be beneficial, but only through self-restraint in their use. Their allocation must be very gradual. To that end the continued use of reserve currencies is essential.

It is equally essential to strengthen the foundations of the inverted pyramid of the international credit structure through securing much larger holdings of monetary gold. This end could be achieved by increasing substantially the price of gold in terms of SDR units. In addition to writing up the book value of existing gold reserves, it would lead to de-hoarding on a large scale and to an increase of the current output. The possession of a substantial monetary gold stock would come to inspire more confidence in reserve currencies and in SDRs, a consideration which enthusiastic advocates of the system should not overlook.

The main object of this book is to point out the hitherto overlooked all-important fact that there is no conflict of interests between those radical reformers who want SDRs to supersede other forms of reserves and those traditionalists who would prefer to retain gold and foreign currencies for reserve purposes. Should extreme reformists have their way and should an attempt be made to replace gold and currencies almost entirely by SDRs, the inevitable outcome would be a disastrous failure. Orthodox believers in gold and in the gold exchange standard, for their part, would serve their cause better if they were prepared to make concessions in favour of a limited but gradually increasing use of SDRs to supplement gold and currencies. The two policies should be complementary to each other.

It is because I believe that sooner or later common sense will prevail that I can foresee a possibility for a revival of the international role of the dollar to follow its present eclipse – always provided that the American people will undergo a national regeneration and their best qualities will assert themselves. The realignment of parities, agreed upon in December 1971, provided an opportunity for this. The question is, will the American nation make use of this opportunity?

CHAPTER THREE

The Rise of the Dollar

FROM the establishment of the gold standard in Britain soon
after the end of the Napoleonic Wars until the beginning of the
First World War sterling's supremacy as the world's leading
currency was uncontested. The pound enjoyed universal confidence all over the five continents and served as the principal
international reserve currency apart from gold, vehicle currency
for international trade, and international standard of value.
Compared with sterling the dollar played a secondary role
before the First World War. Indeed it ranked even behind some
of the leading continental currencies, for it took a long time to
overcome the effects of the Civil War and of the frequent major
economic crises in the United States. Nevertheless, in spite of
the absence of an efficiently organised banking and currency
system – the Federal Reserve did not come into being until 1914
– the importance of the dollar increased during the late 19th
century and the early 20th century, simultaneously with
the spectacular economic growth achieved by the United
States.

Had it not been for the beneficial financial effects of the
neutrality of the United States during the early part of the two
World Wars, and for the immunity of the United States from
the destruction wrought by these wars in Europe, it would have
taken much longer for the dollar to achieve even equality with
sterling, let alone supremacy over it. It is difficult for a generation which has been brought up under the reign of the dollar to
realise that its ultimate victory over sterling had not been a
walkover but the result of a prolonged contest.

The outbreak of the First World War did not automatically
bring the reign of sterling to an end and did not replace it with

the reign of the dollar as soon as Britain became involved in the war in a big way. Indeed in August 1914 sterling rose to a sharp premium over the dollar and continued to remain at a premium until January 1915.

Thereafter, it is broadly true to say that until the middle '60s sterling and the dollar constituted between them a system of duopoly. Even though the dollar was superior to sterling most of the time, and at times considerably superior, sterling continued to hold its own as one of the world's two leading currencies. Their relative importance varied widely, and it differed at any given moment in respect of their various functions. Long after sterling's role as a reserve currency in the countries of the Sterling Area came to be reduced through policies of diversification, it continued to play an important part as a vehicle currency for international trade and as an international standard of value. The dollar was of course incomparably stronger. But sterling continued to be used for foreign trade and for short-term investment.

It was widely believed during the First World War and for a long time after that the redistribution of the European monetary gold stock, accumulated in Fort Knox largely as a result of the American export surpluses, was only a question of time. In reality the process of redistribution did not begin until the '50s. During earlier decades, in time of peace as well as in time of war, the westward flow of gold continued, with only temporary interruptions.

The dollar was progressing from strength to strength most of the time in the inter-war period as well as during the World Wars.

This had not been altogether the result of any deliberate American monetary policy aiming at the achievement and maintenance of the supremacy of the dollar, but largely of America's growing industrial capacity. It is true, until well after the Second World War, the United States prevented debtor countries from repaying their liabilities in goods. But American protectionism was not an instrument of monetary policy. It aimed at safeguarding domestic producers, not at further strengthening the dollar – which was strong enough anyhow – or at attracting even more gold.

Indeed, so far from aiming at increasing deliberately the gold reserve, in both World Wars generous American financial aid to European associates of the United States reduced by many billions the increase of the monetary gold reserve of the United States. After the Second World War American financial assistance continued in various forms on an unprecedented scale, and this time American assistance was not confined to Europe but was world-wide. Together with official encouragement of large-scale export of American private capital during the '50s and the '60s, this generous financial aid was largely responsible for the turn of the tide, leading to a redistribution of American gold among Western European countries.

Although during the First World War the dollar gained ascendancy over sterling, its supremacy came to be challenged at later stages of the war by currencies of countries which remained neutral after the United States entered the war. It was challenged also by the yen because, although Japan was technically a belligerent, her actual participation in the war of 1914 remained purely nominal so that she had been able to retain all the economic advantages of neutral countries. While the dollar was at a premium against sterling (its premium would have been much higher if the rate had not been pegged through official support financed largely by inter-Allied loans) it went to a discount in relation to the currencies of the Scandinavian countries, Spain, Chile, Japan, etc.

Soon after the end of the First World War, in March 1919, inter-Allied financial support and the pegging of exchanges was abandoned and the superiority of the dollar came to assert itself. It rose to a substantial premium, this time not only in relation to the former belligerent countries – including Japan – but also in relation to the currencies of the former neutral countries, because the degree of their post-war inflation exceeded that of the United States. The dollar achieved supremacy as the world's strongest currency.

It was a change, however, which Britain was not prepared to

accept uncontested. All post-war Governments pursued a policy
aimed at enabling sterling to 'look the dollar in the face'. At the
cost of immense sacrifices in the form of handicapping exports
and aggravating the deflationary depression that followed the
short-lived post-war boom, sterling was raised to its old parity.
The gold standard was restored in 1925. It was widely expected
that, as a result of this, even though sterling's supremacy over the
dollar might never return, the superiority of London's financial
facilities would ensure at any rate a sterling–dollar duopoly.
This in spite of the immense superiority of the dollar's strength
due to the possession of a large and increasing gold reserve
and to the effortless maintenance of an almost uninterrupted
balance of payments surplus, in sharp contrast with the
frequently recurrent weakness of sterling, not to speak of the
perennial difficulties of the currencies of France and other
former belligerents.

In spite of this contrast, it was widely assumed in Britain and
elsewhere that sterling would continue to share with the dollar
the role of the leading world currency. Indeed doubts were
entertained in many quarters on both sides of the Atlantic
about the permanent character of the immense financial
superiority of the United States to its full extent. During the
early post-war years the Americans themselves openly voiced
their conviction that the United States was merely holding in
trust the gold acquired from Europe during and immediately
after the war, and that in due course the gold would be re-
turned to its rightful owners. In Britain it was a standing joke
in the early '20s that when a schoolboy, in reply to his teacher's
question what the capital of Europe was, answered unhesita-
tingly: 'New York', his teacher said to him: 'I asked you *what*
the capital of Europe was, not *where* it was.' When in 1926 I paid
a visit to the Federal Reserve Bank of New York and the sight of
large piles of gold in its vaults induced me to quote that joke,
my hosts, Mr Pierre Jay and Mr Randolph Burgess, were
evidently not amused. For by that time the idea of ever
restoring to Europe the gold accumulated in the United States
had become definitely unfashionable.

I was much more popular in American circles when I quoted, with reference to their treasurers in Fort Knox, Edmund Spenser's *Faerie Queene*, describing Mammon's Cave:

'Round about him stood on every side
Greate heapes of golde *that never could be spent.*'   (My italics.)

It did seem for a long time as if gold movements across the Atlantic had become a permanent one-way traffic and that the United States would never have occasion to redistribute her gold hoard.

From the middle of the '20s the influx of gold resulting from the strength of the American balance of payments came to be reinforced by the influx of foreign capital attracted by the upward trend in Wall Street and by the higher interest rates paid for brokers' loans financing the speculative Stock Exchange boom. During the same period on frequent occasions sterling was barely able to hold its own. Nevertheless, London's unique money market facilities and the special relationship between Britain and her world Empire ensured the survival of sterling as a good second international currency to the dollar. Even that position came to be challenged by the French franc for a short time after its stabilisation in 1926. The Reichsmark, benefiting by the overdose of foreign loans and credits obtained by Germany, made a bid for recovering its pre-1914 international importance. Nevertheless, sterling alone continued to share with the dollar the role of a world currency. But its inferiority to the dollar became increasingly obvious in the late '20s.

The Wall Street slump of 1929 and the resulting exodus of foreign long-term and short-term capital from the United States put the dollar on the defensive. Its difficulties became aggravated by the series of bank suspensions that accompanied the slump, and by the prolonged economic depression. The reason why in spite of this the dollar retained its supremacy was that sterling and most other currencies were affected even more than the dollar by the world-wide economic and financial difficulties.

London's main advantage over New York was the soundness of its banks. While American banks closed down by the thousand in the early '30s, there was not a single British bank failure. Many non-residents held on to their sterling because they trusted British banks more than any other banks, even though they did not trust sterling altogether.

The supreme test came after the suspension of the Credit-anstalt in May 1931 and the resulting banking crisis in Germany. Although the United States was affected by the freezing of German credits at the same time as Britain was affected she was in a stronger position to weather the storm. There was a run on sterling which led to the suspension of the gold standard by Britain in September 1931. For the time being sterling appeared to have abandoned its role as a world currency and the dollar reigned supreme.

The depreciation and undervaluation of sterling, together with the aggravation of the economic depression in the United States and the large number of American bank failures, made the dollar increasingly vulnerable, however. It became the main target of speculation most of the time in 1932. With the advent of Roosevelt in the White House it came to be assumed that he would adopt inflationary policies and it was feared that he might follow Britain in suspending the gold standard. This he did in March 1933 as a result of a sweeping flight from the dollar. Both sterling and the dollar became gambling counters of speculators, and for a time there was a monetary power-vacuum. There was no currency whose stability could be relied upon. For, even though the French franc and a few other continental currencies remained stable in terms of gold, their stability became increasingly precarious.

An attempt to restabilise the currencies by common accord at the London Economic Conference in 1933 having failed, the dollar was officially devalued by 41 per cent in 1934. Its new gold parity wax fixed at the fateful figure of $35. But its actual exchange value continued to fluctuate and its fluctuations were influenced by official interventions by both the United States and Britain. The growing volume of international trade during the second half of the '30s was financed by both currencies, with the aid of forward exchange facilities to cover the exchange

risk. The two currencies shared the leadership in the international monetary sphere in spite of their instability, while the
franc and other currencies of the 'gold bloc' lost ground in spite
of their stability because of the growing distrust in the maintenance of their gold parities.

The devaluation of the French franc and of other currencies
in 1936, and the conclusion of the Tripartite Agreement
between the United States, Britain and France in order to
restore monetary stability, failed to restore confidence and the
exchanges continued to fluctuate. From time to time sterling
rose to a premium against the dollar. But gradually during the
late '30s the dollar regained its supremacy, owing to increasing
war fears in Europe, leading to a flight of capital to the United
States, and to increasing expenditure on rearmament. Indeed
such was the confidence in the dollar's strength that during 1937
there was a wave of speculation (the 'gold scare') about the
possibility of a revaluation of the dollar through a reduction of
the gold price from $35. The idea was dropped – if it was ever
entertained seriously – by official American quarters as soon as
they came to realise the extent to which the mere possibility of
such a change was threatening the recovery of American trade
and of world trade after the gradual recovery from the prolonged depression.

Immediately after the outbreak of the Second World War,
Britain devalued sterling to $4·03. The official rate was fixed at
the figure for the duration. The dollar achieved uncontested
superiority, a fact which was indicated by the large discount on
sterling in the unofficial foreign exchange markets in neutral
countries.

With the occupation of practically the whole of Western
Europe by Germany, and even more after the entry of the
United States in the war in 1941, foreign exchange dealings in
markets came to a virtual standstill for the duration of the war.
Inter-Allied transactions were financed mainly with the aid
of Lend-Lease arrangements, while transactions with neutral
countries, mainly in Latin America, were financed largely with
dollars which went to a moderate discount in relation to some

neutral currencies. Even so, the growing economic strength and prestige of the United States and her immunity from enemy occupation or devastation reinforced and consolidated the superiority of the dollar and its leading position as the world currency.

That superiority enabled the United States virtually to dictate her terms in the negotiations that led to the Bretton Woods Agreement, establishing the post-war international monetary system practically on American terms. Those terms ensured that war-time stability of exchange rates should continue and weaker countries relinquished their right to defend their economies with the aid of unlimited currency depreciations or of discriminatory trade or exchange measures against the United States. They also ensured that the stable post-war monetary system would not mean a return to the gold standard but the adoption of the dollar standard. Under it, exchange fluctuations were no longer limited by the gold points – the rates at which it became profitable to ship gold instead of buying or selling foreign exchanges – but by their support points fixed not in relation to their gold parities but in relation to their dollar parities. Central Banks of countries adhering to the IMF were under obligation to maintain their exchanges within these support points. What was even more important, the dollar came to be adopted as the sole intervention currency – the currency which Central Banks had to buy or sell in their operations aimed at maintaining their national currencies within support points.

Keynes and his brilliant team of British negotiators fought a determined rearguard action to safeguard the interests of Britain and of other countries which had been placed in a weak bargaining position by their need for American financial support. But if they made any efforts to ensure the restoration of sterling's pre-war position in the international monetary system as distinct from its position within the Sterling Area they were wholly unsuccessful in that respect. The Bretton Woods Agreement was an official recognition of the dollar's absolute supremacy.

This did not mean that sterling ceased to play an important international role when the Bretton Woods system came to be applied. Thanks to London's highly developed monetary mechanism and to the continued existence of the Sterling Area, sterling was able to hold its own for many years as an important international means of payment, standard of value and reserve currency favoured by many official and unofficial holders. The international monetary system was still one of duopoly, with sterling playing the part of the junior partner. But it gradually drifted towards the monopolistic position of the dollar.

CHAPTER FOUR

The Reign of the Dollar

To set definite datelines for the beginning and end of the period during which the dollar reigned as the supreme currency of the free world and its supremacy was above suspicion would be gross oversimplification. We saw in the last chapter that its progress towards supremacy had been a very gradual process, interrupted from time to time by setbacks. To some extent sterling held its own, notwithstanding Britain's inter-war and post-war difficulties, as a rival to the dollar. Until 1967 a large proportion of world trade continued to be transacted in sterling, even though its importance as a reserve currency declined. The resumption in 1958 of full convertibility of non-resident sterling and of a number of other currencies stimulated activity in the London foreign exchange market. Right until 1967 most foreign exchange business in continental financial centres was based on the sterling cross rate with the foreign currencies transacted. Nevertheless, the supremacy of the dollar was uncontested. It progressed from strength to strength in spite of occasional setbacks such as the one caused by the Korean War.

London's position as an entrepôt trade centre ensured the extensive use of sterling even after it ceased to command sufficient confidence to play a leading role outside the Sterling Area as a private and public reserve currency. The existence of excellent forward exchange facilities in London enabled holders of sterling balances to cover their exchange risk. And since London remained the world's best foreign exchange market this alone made the continued use of sterling by overseas bankers and merchants necessary.

In the course of the '60s the development of various new

short-term borrowing and investment facilities in London provided additional inducement for holding sterling, whenever it
was profitable to do so, allowing for the cost of covering the
exchange risk. Owing to the Labour Government's ill-advised
policy of defending sterling by means of supporting the forward
rate at an artificially overvalued level, it was for years very
cheap to cover the exchange risk on sterling. Thanks to this,
sterling's international role was prolonged in spite of the decline
of the extent to which it inspired confidence abroad. This was
inconsistent with the Government's declared policy of aiming
at relinquishing sterling's international role for the sake of
protecting the domestic economy from the effects of large-
scale withdrawals of foreign funds whenever the Government abstained from adopting confidence-inspiring measures.

Progress towards the supremacy of the dollar received
powerful support from a most unexpected quarter. General de
Gaulle's hostility towards the United States was fully equalled
by his hostility to Britain. And since sterling was more vulnerable than the dollar he concentrated his main attacks on the
former, much as he must have disliked to strengthen thereby
the relative position of the dollar. When he vetoed Britain's
admission into the EEC unless sterling ceased to be an international currency it became the openly declared policy of the
Labour Government, and also the Conservative Government
that succeeded it, to divest sterling from the remnants of its
former role as a reserve currency. Up to the time of writing this
declaration of intent has not been fully implemented, even
though in 1971, on the occasion of the renewal of the Basle
arrangement of 1968 for the guarantee of official Sterling Area
sterling balances, there was an all-round cut of 10 per cent of
the minimum limits for Sterling Area balances in London.

The survival of sterling's international role to a limited extent
was only one of the reasons why the reign of the dollar in the
'50s and the '60s was not altogether complete. Another reason
was the emergence of currencies which became from time to
time stronger than the dollar – the Deutschemark, the Swiss
franc, the French franc, the yen and some other currencies.

Fortunately from the point of view of the dollar's ambition to reign supreme, none of the countires concerned harboured similar ambitions, or even ambitions to share with the dollar the role of a world currency. From time to time their strength (or the dollar's periodically recurrent weakness) led to a wholesale flight of funds into these currencies and as a result dollar scares developed. But these passing phenomena – to be dealt with in greater detail in the next chapter – failed to affect the basic supremacy of the dollar, secured by the rules of the Bretton Woods system and by the growing industrial strength of the United States.

As we saw in the last chapter the United States had virtually dictated the rules of the IMF in such a way as to establish the dollar standard. This ambition was reinforced by the growing supremacy of the American economy and by the growing influence of American business in European industries. It was the official policy to maintain and strengthen this supremacy. For this purpose among others the United States Government was generous – indeed some would say over-generous – in distributing gifts and loans abroad. This enabled overseas countries to buy American goods and to cover their deficits arising from their inability to sell to the United States as much as they were buying from her. The unwritten formula was 'aid not trade', as a result of which it was the American tax-payer who financed over a period of many years a very large part of the American export surpluses.

The process of financial aid in time of peace began soon after the end of the War with the large billion pound loan to Britain, which was granted on the condition that sterling was to be made convertible for foreign holders of sterling balances. Considering that in 1946 the world was starving for dollars and had a surfeit of unwanted sterling, the inevitable consequence of this arrangement was that the United States was really financing the purchases of American goods by the five continents – under British guarantee. At that time Britain was the only country which America trusted, so instead of taking higher risk by lending to less trustworthy countries, she enabled them to import American goods by lending to Britain and making her convert the dollar proceeds to foreign holders of sterling. This 'aid not trade' move was followed later by the Marshall Aid, which was much more generous and much less businesslike – 'the most unsordid act in history' according to Churchill. But it reduced the incentive for beneficiary countries to make an adequate effort to work out their own salvation.

Economic and military aid continued throughout the '50s and the '60s. Judging by the decline of the American gold reserve and by the increase of American foreign short-term liabilities, she gave away much more than she could afford to give away. At the same time, private long-term lending abroad, which came virtually to an end during the crises that followed the Wall Street slump, gradually revived. It was very selective, as the number of countries which commanded sufficient confidence to attract private investors was relatively small. The extent of assistance through this channel was very considerable however, and it continued for many years after the American balance of payments no longer had enough surplus to export so much capital. At that time the New York market for foreign issue was virtually the only capital market open for foreign issues. Although it was of great assistance for European countries with a high credit rating and for other privileged borrowers who were able to meet their capital requirements and foreign exchange requirements, like Marshall Aid it delayed the effort of the borrowing countries to regain their self-sufficiency. Moreover, the efficiency of the New York capital market and its apparently inexhaustible resources discouraged the development of rival capital markets in the borrowing countries or in intermediary centres.

Not until towards the middle '60s did the United States authorities discover that they could not afford to remain the sole major capital market in the world. Accordingly in 1964 they adopted measures to discourage foreign issues in New York. Foremost amongst them was the 15 per cent Interest Equalisation Tax imposed on all medium- and long-term foreign issues in the United States, with the exception of those issued by certain privileged countries. The result was that the European financial centres had to revert, willy-nilly, to their pre-war role of meeting at least their own requirements, but also those of other European and other confidence-inspiring countries. Since London could not afford to export British capital it assumed the role of intermediary by participating in the issue of foreign Euro-bonds placed in other countries – with non-resident holdings of sterling.

Such was the world-wide confidence in the superior strength of the dollar that its leadership remained taken for granted in spite of the progressive decline of the American gold reserve and the increase of American short-term and long-term indebtedness abroad. Simultaneously with the export of American capital in the absence of an export surplus available for that purpose, United States firms with affiliates abroad were encouraged to cover their capital requirements abroad. At the same time the import of foreign long-term capital was encouraged.

The strength of the dollar was not absolute but relative, since it was largely due to the weakness of other currencies, especially of sterling. On innumerable occasions the British Government asked for, and received, American financial help on a large scale. Although the rescue operations in each crisis between 1964 and 1969 were international arrangements with the participation of a number of countries, on each occasion the United States took a leading part in them. Likewise when the lira or the franc got into trouble in the '60s, the United States was ready to play her part in the salvage, although by that time the dollar itself came under a cloud from time to time.

Even though New York was no longer able to fulfil the role of the world's international capital market and the United States had to re-borrow capital she exported abroad, the dollar continued to be regarded as the focal point of the monetary system. This was largely due to the progressive weakening of sterling. Owing to the frequently recurrent sterling crises, especially under the Labour Government, sterling was under a cloud both before and after its devaluation in 1967. That devaluation marked the end of the sterling–dollar duopoly. By abandoning the defence of its parity the British Government conceded defeat. While the devaluation of 1949 was an adjustment which restored confidence in sterling at its lower level, the devaluation of 1967 left sterling under a cloud, owing to the delay of its effect on the balance of payments.

That is was no longer suitable to play a leading part in the international monetary system was indicated by the fact that, from the devaluation, in the London market foreign currencies came to be dealt in almost entirely on the basis of their cross rates with the dollar. In continental centres, too, this method of dealing was adopted to replace the well-established practice of most continental markets to deal in foreign currencies other than sterling on the basis of their quotations in terms of sterling. Even though the method of quoting sterling in London in terms of foreign currencies instead of quoting foreign currencies in terms of sterling continued to exist, actual dealing took place mostly on the basis of their dollar cross rates. This change was rather more than a mere technicality. It amounted to the realisation and admission that the pound had lost its former role as the leading intermediary currency for the purpose of conducting foreign exchange operations. That role came to be assumed by the dollar. This did not mean, however, that London's role as the leading foreign exchange market ended or even declined. Owing to the difference between business hours in New York and all European foreign exchange markets London continues to be the centre through which most foreign exchange transactions are still concluded in spite of the decline in the international role of sterling in other respects.

Another consequence of the devaluation and its failure to restore confidence in sterling has been the sharp decline in the role of sterling as a currency for invoicing and for financing international trade. Until 1967 a great deal of trade between non-British countries within and outside the Sterling Area was transacted in terms of sterling. But the termination of the official support of forward sterling following on the disastrous experience of losses suffered by the Exchange Equalisation Account through the devaluation of 1967 made it too costly for many creditors in sterling to cover their claims through forward transactions. Accordingly most exporters outside the U.K. – including those of the Outer Sterling Area – came to transact their foreign trade in terms of dollars. Even many U.K. firms were prepared to quote in dollar or accept quotations in dollars.

This again did not affect London's position as the principal foreign exchange market. Quite on the contrary, since a high proportion of British imports and exports were now quoted in dollars the exchange took place in London instead of in foreign centres. But it did increase the importance of the dollar as the principal international currency.

Sterling's international role was further reduced within the Sterling Area also as a result of the Basle Agreement concluded in 1968, providing for an international guarantee of the dollar value of a high proportion of official sterling balances of the countries of the Sterling Area, in return for an undertaking not to withdraw a certain percentage of these balances. This was part of the policy to divest sterling of its international role in order to satisfy France.

The way in which politicians, Treasury officials and Central Bankers of various nations are in the habit of discussing in all seriousness across the conference table whether this currency or that currency should or should not be an international currency is indeed amazing as well as amusing. As if it were they, and not the markets and the public which either trusts a currency or distrusts it, who could determine the international role of a currency. This attitude recalls the pronouncement made by Emperor William II towards the close of 1899 that the twentieth century was to begin on 1 January, 1900. As if the facts of simple arithmetic, by which the first century A.D. ended on 31 December A.D. 100, and the nineteenth century must end therefore, on 31 December 1900, could be altered by Imperial decree! It is equally absurd, though unfortunately less obviously so, to try to settle by negotiation between Governments and Central Banks that henceforth sterling or the dollar must cease to be an international currency. A currency is used for international purposes if it is trusted abroad.

Of course Governments and Central Banks can decide

whether it can be bought, sold or held on official account. Drastic exchange control can also prevent or discourage the use of a currency for international purposes by the private sector of the economies. But in the absence of such action a currency is used as an international currency if it is trusted, regardless of official views on the subject.

This was how the situation actually developed after the attempt to deprive sterling of the last remains of its international role. And this is what will happen in respect of the dollar regardless of any official decisions to replace it by SDR, which in any case can only be used by the authorities.

After the return of some degree of confidence in sterling in 1969–71 many countries of the Outer Sterling Area increased their sterling balances well in excess of the amount guaranteed in terms of dollars. In any case, international confidence in dollars declined in the meantime, and the value of a dollar guarantee of the sterling balances came to be looked upon as problematic. Nevertheless, the conclusion of the arrangement in 1968 indicated a further admission of the superiority of the dollar.

Indeed, by 1968 the dollar became the universally recognised reserve currency, given the fact that even much of the surviving sterling reserves had to be given a dollar guarantee. International trade between third countries came to be transacted mostly in terms of dollars. Owing to the increasing use of Euro-dollar facilities it also came to be financed very largely in terms of dollars in spite of the efforts of the United States authorities to discourage the granting of dollar credits to foreign borrowers by banks resident in the United States.

By the time the dollar achieved total victory over sterling other currencies emerged which were considered stronger than the dollar. The Deutschemark was at a perennial premium against the dollar and so, most of the time, was the Swiss franc. But, as already observed, both the West German and the Swiss Governments aimed at discouraging the international use of their currencies by stopping the payment of interest on foreign deposits and by other devices. In the case of Switzerland the ban was not statutory but was based on a 'gentleman's agreement' between banks. None the less it was largely effective, and in 1971 it was made statutory.

For some time in the late '60s the French franc came to be considered the strongest currency, and it was General de Gaulle's intention to encourage its international use by removing exchange controls early in 1968, to prepare the ground for its extensive international use as a means for causing additional embarrassment to the dollar. This in addition to his efforts to discredit and weaken the dollar by converting into gold most of the Bank of France's dollar holdings and by trying to incite other Governments to act likewise. He presumably hoped that as a result of creating a free market in Paris a strong convertible franc, backed with a big gold reserve, would stand a better chance to compete with the dollar as an international currency. But the disturbances of May–June 1968 put the franc on the defensive and France had to depend once more on international financial support. This was given with the generous participation of the United States, in spite of the recent active anti-American moves of General de Gaulle in the monetary sphere.

After the abortive attempt to set up the franc as a rival currency, the dollar appeared to be riding high and its supremacy appeared to be beyond question for a while, in spite of the occasional rush into Deutschemarks in anticipation of its re-valuation. Yet by the concluding years of the '60s the dollar's inherent weakness was becoming increasingly obvious. A period of decline evidently set in. It was just as gradual as the rise of the dollar to supremacy had been. For a long time after the dollar has passed the peak of its power it continued to be regarded as the main international currency. But it was living largely on its old reputation.

The dollar standard, which was the world's monetary system until 1971, arose from the terms of the Bretton Woods system and its application in the rules of the IMF. But owing to the weakening of the dollar's basic strength and to the superior strength of more than one other currency, it became an anachronistic anomaly by the '70s.

CHAPTER FIVE

Decline of the Dollar's Supremacy

OWING to the immense economic, political and military power and prestige of the United States the decline of the dollar's supremacy was not widely realised for a long time after her financial power passed its peak. The world had grown used to look upon the dollar as the symbol of financial strength as a matter of course. Until 15 August 1971 there was no sudden shock comparable with the devaluation of sterling in 1967, which would have made the world realise the fundamental change in the situation. In fact, the dollar was able to live on its old reputation for a long time. Its decline was a very gradual insidious process, and even many of those who ought to have known better were reluctant to believe that it had ceased to have the strength for dominating the financial world.

Paradoxically enough, the process of underlying decay set in long before the public progress of the dollar towards supremacy reached its climax. The weakness of sterling disguised the basic weakness of the dollar for a long time, diverting from it the speculative pressure to which it would have been subject as a result of a series of adverse balances of payments, if sterling had not monopolised the speculators' attention. In any case, in spite of the persistent decline of the American gold reserve in the late '50s and in the '60s, the United States had until 1971 the largest gold and foreign exchange reserve, and she still holds the largest monetary gold stock. What received less attention than the decline of the American gold reserve, even though it was equally important, was the extent to which foreign dollar balances were mounting up. By 1971 their total – not counting foreign long-term investments, even though a high proportion of these, too, could easily be converted into liquid non-resident balances – rose to something like five times the amount of the gold reserve. Official dollar holdings alone, which were supposed to be freely convertible into gold until 15 August, 1971, were about three times the amount of the gold reserve.

The United States changed her former role of perennial lender to that of perennial borrower. She incurred heavy liabilities in relation to the IMF, and it was largely under American pressure that SDRs were adopted, largely for the sake of enabling the United States as well as Britain to borrow even more. From time to time the United States had to draw extensively on reciprocal swap facilities arranged with a large number of Central Banks. She also placed non-marketable short-term and medium-term Treasury paper with some Central Banks. Simultaneously there was an increase in foreign holdings of American long-term Government loans which were held almost exclusively by foreign Treasuries and Central Banks.

Private portfolio investments and direct investments in the United States, too, constituted a potential source of pressure on the dollar. Admittedly, on the other side of the balance sheet there was an increase of American long-term investments abroad. But their total could not be deducted from that of foreign assets in the United States. For when the dollar comes under acute pressure American residents are not likely to liquidate their holdings to provide foreign exchanges to meet the selling pressure on the dollar.

In the late '6os the United States acquired the habit of borrowing heavily in the Euro-dollar market, mainly through foreign branches of American banks, which re-lent the proceeds to their head offices. At the same time her long-term borrowing in the Euro-bond market – mainly in the form of bonds convertible into equities – reached formidable proportions.

The decline of the inherent strength of the dollar did not prevent the United States from rushing to the rescue of sterling and other currencies whenever they got into acute difficulties. This was partly because generosity had become a habit and partly because, while she could ill afford to support other currencies, she could also ill afford not to support them. A devaluation of a major currency such as sterling would have reacted on the dollar. This was what actually occurred after the devaluation of sterling, which triggered off a large-scale speculative and hoarding demand for gold in the free gold market. Under the Central Banks' Gold Pool arrangement the free market was supported to keep the price in the vicinity of the official American price. The lion's share in the burden of this exercise fell on the United States and she suffered heavy losses of gold during the concluding months of 1967 and in the early part of 1968.

Although the American authorities were urged from all sides to give up pouring gold into the bottomless pit of the free market with its immense hoarding demand and speculative demand, they stubbornly refused to heed the advice, pledging themselves repeatedly to the defence of the market price of gold 'to the last dollar'. Fortunately, long before they exhausted their gold reserve in accordance with this senseless pledge, common sense came to prevail, and the Central Banks' Gold Pool was discontinued. The price of gold in the free market was allowed to find its own level, but the United States used all her influence on the IMF to induce the latter to lay down rules preventing Central Banks from buying gold in the free market or re-selling gold withdrawn from the United States at the official price. The establishment of the 'two-tier' system of gold prices enabled the United States to recover some of the gold lost earlier, because speculative short positions in dollars were covered and speculative accounts in gold bought against dollars were closed as and when the market price was rising.

One of the main reasons for the deterioration of the position of the dollar was the war in Vietnam. This aspect of the dollar crisis had all the elements of tragedy. The war proved to be more prolonged and more costly than had been expected, and it added very considerably to the one-sided sacrifices made by the United States to fulfil her role as the main defender of the free world. Compared with her share in the cost of maintaining adequate military forces to deter imperialist-Communist aggression, the contributions of other members of NATO and of SEATO were negligible.

Germany and Japan, having been disarmed as a result of their defeat, showed no inclination to rearm to any considerable extent, in the secure knowledge that they were now under the protection of the nuclear shield of the United States. While Germany derived much financial benefit from the presence of Allied forces, Japan also benefited financially by her neutrality in the wars in Korea and in Vietnam. All the time the United States used up a large part of her financial strength by carrying a disproportionate share of the free man's burden.

To the extent to which the decline of the strength of the dollar was attributable to this cause it was grossly unfair to the United States. The exorbitant cost of foreign aid (Mr Nixon gave the figure of 143 billion dollars as their grand total since 1945) also largely contributed towards the weakening of the dollar. But while expenditure on the military defences of the free world was an inevitable sacrifice made for safeguarding the freedom of the free world – Allies as well as uncommitted nations – much of the expenditure on foreign aid might well have been saved. Too much of America's financial strength was expended on nations which deemed it their birthright to bite the hand that fed them – before, during and after feeding. The United States received no thanks for these billions which should have been reserved for maintaining the strength of the dollar. Even much of the aid given to allied nations was grossly premature. The financial ammunition of the United States was used up before the enemy came within firing range.

Mr Nixon and other Americans can hardly be blamed for feeling bitter about the way European countries and Japan became rich at the expense of the United States, largely thanks to their inadequate contribution to the burden of defending the free world. It took too long for the United States Governments that succeeded each other in the post-war period to realise that their friends and allies could now well afford to devote more of their resources to national defence instead of raising their standard of living while the United States bore more than her fair share of the military expenditure of the free world. The moment Western European countries and Japan began to accumulate reserves well beyond their immediate requirements the Washington Administration could have discontinued financial and military aid unless these countries agreed to contribute their due share of the military expenditure.

But to a very large extent the decline of the financial power of the United States was entirely her own fault. To the extent to which the loss of reserves was due to over-exporting capital she has only herself to blame. This subject will be dealt with in greater detail in Chapter 9 on 'Dollar-imperialism'. It denounces the Americans' short-sightedness in trying to buy up the industries of advanced countries, very much against the wishes of some of the peoples and Governments concerned. This 'invasion' was financed largely through using up the gold reserve, thereby weakening the defences of the dollar and reducing the financial, political and military influence of the United States in the world. Excessive export of American capital continued even after the gold reserve was reduced to what was considered to be the country's minimum requirements. It was financed partly through increasing the external short-term indebtedness of the United States, and later through raising the necessary capital in Europe. Possibly the United States stood to benefit in the long run through the yield on these foreign investments – which is in fact a substantial item on the credit side – and also to the extent to which it would be repatriated. Their capital appreciation of these investments was also highly beneficial. But the immediate effect of the heavy outflow of capital was one of the causes of the decline of the financial power of the United States. Instead of being able to continue to assist others she placed herself in an inferior position in which she was herself in frequent need of assistance. The dollar, having been the strongest and safest currency for so long, had to be looked upon as one of the weakest and most vulnerable among the currencies of advanced industrial countries.

Short-sighted politicians might conceivably have allowed the dollar's defences to weaken even further, had it not been for the firm stand taken by the Pentagon. Military leaders succeeded in making the Administration realise that national security required the maintenance of a minimum gold reserve of at least $10 billion for financing overseas military bases and military operations abroad. There is reason to believe that it was largely under the influence of the Pentagon that the Treasury decided in March 1968 to stop pouring American gold down the drain by continuing to try to satisfy the insatiable requirements of hoarders and speculators at the price of $35 per ounce. The bigoted dogmatists of the United States Treasury had seriously believed that speculative demand would be bound to come to an end long before the American gold stock would become exhausted. After the loss of each billion the politicians in Washington and their expert advisers were firmly convinced that surely there was no longer sufficient capital available for financing more gold purchases. Remarks to that effect could and should be listed among the 'famous last words'.

Once the Gold Pool operations came to an end the free market price of gold rose sharply. The resulting discrepancy between the official price of gold and the free market price became one of the indications of the basic weakness of the dollar. It was not allowed, however, to indicate the full extent of the true value of gold. Through American influence with the IMF to manipulate its rules, official operations in the free market were discouraged. Largely as a result of this, the premium on the free market price of gold was brought down for a short time to vanishing point, especially as the exorbitant costs of financing hoarded gold with the aid of borrowed money at high interest rates induced many holders to take their profits. But in due course the premium reappeared, indicating the consensus of market opinion that a devaluation of the dollar was a mere question of time.

Another effort made by the American authorities to check the decline of the dollar's supremacy was the adoption of various exchange control measures, first in the form of unofficial 'guidelines' and later in the form of statutory restrictions. In doing so the United States reversed its basic policy aimed at the liberalisation of international finance. This confirmed the view that only economically strong countries could really afford to be liberal. It was not sheer accident that Britain abandoned in the '30s her traditional free trader policy, because she could no longer afford to rely on the unfettered forces of the markets to restore equilibrium by correcting temporary deviations in the course of time. By the '60s the dollar, too, needed artificial defensive measures in the form of exchange controls, aimed at checking the outflow of American capital which by then the United States could ill afford to lose. This restriction affected mainly the issue of foreign bonds in New York.

The reason why the decline of the dollar was delayed and mitigated for a long time was, in addition to sterling's weakness – to which the weakness of the French franc was added after the troubles of 1968 – the efforts of General de Gaulle to induce the British Government to deprive sterling of its role as a reserve currency. Since there was no alternative reserve currency to sterling apart from the dollar, it retained and even increased its role as the foreign currency in which public bodies and private interests accumulated their reserves. It is true, during the '60s it became fashionable to diversify reserves and there were many holding of Deutschemarks, Swiss francs, etc., in spite of the efforts of the Governments concerned to discourage the practice. But the bulk of reserves continued to be transferred into dollars, thanks to which the decline of its basic strength did not become obvious until the concluding years of the decade and, even more, in the opening years of the '70s.

From time to time the decline of the dollar's basic strength became accentuated by flights into Deutschemark or some other revaluation-prone currency. For a long time the resulting selling pressure on the dollar was attributed simply to the inherent strength of the currencies concerned, not to any inherent weakness of the dollar itself. It took some time before it came to be realised that the large-scale buying of Deutschemarks, etc., against the sale of the dollar was due as much to distrust in dollars as to confidence in the currencies concerned.

Worst of all, the very basis of the strength of the dollar became undermined as a result of the spreading of the 'English disease' in the United States. Gradually the American trade unions realised how much the British worker could get away with and they stepped up their wage demands accordingly, regardless of considerations of productivity, the increase of which came virtually to a halt simultaneously with escalating costs. This more than anything else was responsible for the deterioration of the balance of visible trade. Notwithstanding increased unemployment, consumption continued to remain too high in the United States, owing to higher wages.

Admittedly, the inherent weakness of the dollar did not prevent it from continuing to appear to be the leading currency. It was still the principal reserve currency, even though sterling continued to some extent to hold its own. Owing to the Basle guarantees of Sterling Area balances the wholesale withdrawals were checked – in any case there could not have been any, since major demands by large holders would have compelled the British Government to make sterling legally inconvertible. Actually the improvement of Britain's balance of payments and the resulting return of confidence in sterling attracted more Sterling Area balances well above the guaranteed maximum. Even so, taking the world as a whole, sterling's role as a reserve currency remained insignificant compared with the dollar's role, in spite of the decline of confidence in the latter.

CHAPTER SIX

Euro-dollars – A Source of Strength or Weakness?

W E have to interrupt our narrative at this stage for the sake of an important diversion, to examine the part Euro-dollars played in the tragedy of the dollar. One of the reasons why the dollar's international prestige and influence continued to increase even after the progressive decline of its inherent strength was the spectacular expansion of the Euro-dollar market. But opinions are divided whether it was a source of strength for the dollar or a source of weakness. Was the availability of almost inexhaustible supplies of borrowed dollars not one of the main causes of the decline of its strength? It is a question to which we would all like to find an absolutely convincing answer, and over which experts are likely to pursue their inconclusive arguments for generations to come.

One thing is certain and obvious. The availability of large-scale facilities for lending and borrowing in terms of dollars independently of domestic monetary policies in the United States was one of the main attractions of the dollar for non-residents. It is true, there are Euro-currencies – deposits in terms of currencies other than those of the holders – other than Euro-dollars. But the volume of Euro-dollar deposits greatly exceeds the grand total of all other Euro-currencies. The extensive use of dollar holdings in the form of Euro-dollars greatly increased its prestige and it also expanded the sphere in which dollars could be used. But the other side of the picture was the availability of additional billions of dollars for speculative purposes.

For a detailed description of the origin, technique and theory of Euro-dollars I must refer the reader to the latest revised edition of my book *The Euro-Dollar System*. In this chapter we are concerned solely with the question whether and to what extent the Euro-dollar system has helped the dollar to achieve supremacy and to maintain its supremacy even after the decline of its inherent strength.

The practice of lending and borrowing dollar deposits by banks resident outside the United States emerged in the late '50s largely as a result of the restrictions imposed on dollar deposit rates by the American authorities, and of the rigidity of the terms American banks allow to their customers, whether depositors or borrowers. Banks outside the United States – mainly in London but to a less extent also in other financial centres – acquired the habit of borrowing dollar deposits between each other and also outside the market, at rates well above the maximum limits for dollar time deposit fixed in the United States under Regulation Q. The volume of such transactions rose sharply, especially from the late '60s, and in 1971 the outstanding total must have exceeded $60 billion, in spite of the relaxation of Regulation Q and the disappearance or mitigation of some other causes responsible for the expansion of the Euro-dollar market.

There can be no doubt that, just as the adoption and increasing use of sterling acceptances in the late nineteenth century had increased considerably the international prestige of sterling, so the adoption and increasing use of the practice of lending and borrowing Euro-dollar deposits has increased considerably the international prestige of the dollar. To a very large degree Euro-dollars took the place of sterling acceptances. In fact, one of the causes of their increased use was the restrictions imposed in 1957 on the use of sterling acceptance for the financing of non-British international trade and for refinancing transactions. Non-resident holders of dollars found that they were able to lend their dollars outside the United States on terms more favourable than those obtainable in the United States. Keen competition between banks holding Euro-dollars – whether their own dollars or those of their customers – enabled borrowers to obtain better terms. Even residents of the United States got into the habit of lending or borrowing Euro-dollars in large transactions.

Owing to the large size of the London Euro-dollar market and the active turnover in it, it is usually possible to buy and sell substantial amounts without unduly affecting the rates. The terms of borrowing and lending banks are flexible. Euro-dollars can be used in a wide variety of ways, for short-term investment or borrowing, or for speculation, or for arbitrage in time or in space. Because of this and of the possibility of securing more attractive rates than those offered either by banks in the United States or by any of the New York money market instruments, their existence constitutes an inducement for many non-resident holders to retain their holdings even if they have no immediate need for dollars. If the holder hesitates whether to retain his dollars or to switch into some other currency, the additional facilities provided by the Euro-dollar system are liable to influence his decision, at any rate to some slight extent.

Transactions in Euro-dollars entail, in a large number of instances, foreign exchange transactions which tend to broaden the London market in dollars. This itself makes for an increased prestige of the dollar and for an increased need for foreign banks and other firms to maintain holdings of dollars in London. Interest arbitrage is apt to remove from the foreign exchange market large amounts of dollars for the duration of the transactions.

There is, however, another side to the picture. As pointed out above the availability of very large additional supplies of dollars for speculation against the currency must have contributed to no slight extent to the decline of the dollar's supremacy. The existence of tens of billions of Euro-dollar deposits is bound to be a potential source of pressure on the dollar. From the point of view of representing a potential selling pressure the fact that the non-resident holder has sold his dollars to another non-resident need not necessarily increase the likelihood of additional selling pressure. It depends on the purpose for which the original holder and the new holder intended to use the dollars. But the operation of the Euro-dollar system certainly does make additional facilities available for an increase of speculative selling pressure on the dollar. It doubles the extent of that selling pressure if both original owner and new owner take a gloomy view of the prospects of the dollar. The new owner may borrow the dollar deposits for the purpose of selling the proceeds as spot dollars without covering the forward exchange. And the original non-resident owner may sell forward the dollars which he had lent for a definite period, so as to safeguard himself against loss liable to arise from a depreciation of the dollar by the time the deposit matures.

There is another way in which Euro-dollar facilities tended to contribute towards selling pressure on the dollar. The Euro-dollar market enabled importers to lengthen their leads by financing their imports with the aid of borrowed Euro-dollars. This is possible not only when the imports are invoiced in dollars but, thanks to the availability of forward exchange facilities, also when they are payable in other currencies, provided that the forward rate is in their favour. The availability of Euro-dollar facilities tended to lengthen leads, because Euro-dollar deposits, or credits based on them, are now obtainable for much longer periods than those of conventional trade credits or conventional bank credits. Euro-dollars are available for twelve months as a matter of routine, and even for much longer periods. Banks are now able to lend to their customers for periods well beyond the customary three months with the option of one renewal for the same period, because with the aid of Euro-dollar facilities they can easily cover their risk of an increase in interest rates by means of borrowing long-term offsetting deposits at rates current at the time of the transaction. Markets for long-term deposits in terms of currencies other than the dollar are not nearly as good as the Euro-dollar market. This fact goes a long way towards stimulating lending with the aid of dollars. Thanks to Euro-dollar facilities payments due in dollars can thus be deferred for many months, even for years. The foreign exchange market is only affected when the borrower has to buy the dollars in order to repay the borrowed Euro-dollars.

Yet another reason of at least equal importance for the increase of potential selling pressure on the dollar through the operation of the Euro-dollar system is that the American monetary authorities have no means of restricting the speculative sale of Euro-dollars by non-resident holders. Speculators against the dollar have the choice between selling borrowed spot dollars or forward dollars, but the extent of their potential sales of spot dollars held by residents in the United States may be curtailed by credit squeeze or by exchange control measures. On the other hand the American authorities cannot prevent non-resident owners of dollars from selling their holdings. Considering the large size of the total volume of Euro-dollars the inability of the American authorities to control speculative spot sales with the aid of borrowed Euro-dollars either by credit squeeze or by exchange restrictions must make quite an appreciable difference.

The operation of the Euro-dollar system has also weakened the power of the Federal Reserve to pursue a domestic monetary policy which would tend to increase the basic strength of the dollar, curtailing domestic consumption and thereby improving the balance of payments. This end was sought to be achieved in the late '60s by means of credit squeeze. But American banks and big business firms were in a position to circumvent the credit squeeze by borrowing Euro-dollars abroad. This was done on a gigantic scale by branches of American banks in London and in other Euro-dollar markets during 1968–70. These branches re-lent the proceeds to their head offices, enabling the latter to expand credit to their domestic customers in spite of the domestic credit restraint. Or they used the borrowed dollars for financing foreign trade which would have been financed by their head offices. This enabled the latter to increase the volume of credit that was available for domestic financing.

Towards the middle of 1970 the United States authorities did take belated steps aimed at discouraging American borrowing of Euro-dollars. But these measures were far from adequate.

They were merely aimed at preventing or mitigating a further increase in the amount of Euro-dollars borrowed by American bank branches, not to induce them to repay the excessive amounts borrowed earlier. In actual practice they were not even able to prevent a further increase. Since the Federal Reserve imposed reserve requirements on Euro-dollars liabilities, the head offices of American banks felt impelled to borrow even more Euro-dollars through their branches abroad in order to comply with these requirements.

For all practical purposes the London Euro-dollar market became the London branch of the New York money market over a long period. London Euro-dollar rates came to be strongly influenced by various New York interest rates, especially by changes in the prime lending rates of American banks. Owing to the close relationship established by American banks with the Euro-dollar market, the volume of their new borrowings or repayments largely determined Euro-dollar trends. It came to influence interest rates in the local London money markets and also the sterling–dollar exchange rate, both spot and forward. Although by the late '6os the dollar's inherent strength was well on the downward path, this did not prevent it from achieving an unprecedented position of technical supremacy in the international monetary sphere.

This was a curiously anomalous situation. Instead of leading from strength, the dollar came to lead from weakness. It influenced interest rates – and through them exchange rates – not because American banks were the largest lenders who were in a position to impose their terms on borrowers, but because they were the largest borrowers. The extent of American borrowing in London is explained by the high degree of creditworthiness of many American banks, thanks to which they were able to borrow hundreds of millions of dollars in a single day – indeed there were single items of transactions amounting to $100 million or even $150 million. The rates which they were prepared to pay dominated the trend in the market.

A reason why the Euro-dollar market has gone a long way towards endangering international monetary and economic

stability is that it has greatly increased uncontrolled and virtually uncontrollable international liquidity. Of course from
the point of view of those who are convinced that ever-increasing international liquidity must be looked upon in all conceivable circumstances as a Good Thing, and that we could
never have even enough of liquidity, let alone too much of it,
this is a strong point in favour of Euro-dollars. They fail to
realise the immense risk that the existence of $60 billion un-
secured non-self-liquidating Euro-dollar credits represents. A
very high proportion of Euro-dollar deposits is lent and re-lent
quite a number of times before it reaches the ultimate borrower.
If any one of the resulting chain of debtors should default, one
single failure might be followed by a chain of defaults. Apart
altogether from this, there is also the risk – some of us consider it
certainty – of the inflationary effect of excessive liquidity.

One should have thought that the IMF and the Governments behind it would consider it their foremost duty to make
provision enabling them to cope with a major crisis that is
liable to arise from a collapse of the Euro-dollar boom. That
was the kind of crisis for which the creation of SDRs was urged
by some of those advocating it. Instead, their indiscriminate
distribution for the sake of creating unnecessary and unjustified
supplementary liquidity began in 1970 in the middle of
escalating wage inflation, when the expansion of Euro-dollars,
providing additional liquidity, was gathering momentum. The
increased volume of Euro-dollars provided additional means for
selling dollars short and for buying Deutschemarks in anticipation of their revaluation. At the same time it made the inverted
pyramid of international paper credit even more vulnerable.
More will be said about this in Chapter 7.

The use of Euro-dollars as a means for speculating in foreign
exchanges had a strongly self-aggravating effect. A very high
proportion of the dollars borrowed in the Euro-dollar market
was sold against Deutschemarks and other revaluation-prone
currencies, making them even more revaluation-prone. There
appeared to be even more reason for expecting an early devaluation of the dollar or a revaluation of other currencies, or

their upward floating. The landslide-like flight into Deutsche-marks was largely the result of the expansion of the Euro-dollar market. The German authorities, in an attempt to discourage the inflationary effect of the unwanted influx, restricted domestic credit, but this was largely circumvented through German borrowing of Euro-dollars, which again, through causing an increase in Euro-dollar rates, contributed towards the increase in the volume of Euro-dollars.

It seems reasonable to suggest that, but for the existence of almost inexhaustible sources of dollars available for transfer into Deutschemarks, the German Government might not have been forced to allow its currency to float upward and the United States might not have been forced to suspend the con-vertibility of the dollar in August 1971. The question whether these changes were for better or for worse may be a matter of opinion. Here I confine myself to quoting these outstanding instances as an indication of the powerful role Euro-dollars played in undermining international monetary stability created by the Bretton Woods system.

The expansion of the Euro-Deutschemark market, too, contributed indirectly towards the weakening of the dollar, through encouraging the flow of foreign funds into Germany, by enabling foreign holders of Deutschemarks to earn interest on their deposits in spite of the ban imposed on German banks to pay interest on them. Non-resident holders of Deutschemark deposits were able to lend them in the Euro-Deutschemark market on a large scale and, during the period of fantastically high interest rates, at relatively attractive deposit rates. Speculative buyers of Deutschemarks did not have to lose interest, so that they were able to speculate on capital gains through a revaluation of their Deutschemark holdings without forgoing the yield on their funds. This possibility greatly in-creased the demand for Deutschemarks.

Taking everything into consideration, it seems reasonable to conclude that the expansion of the Euro-currency market in general and the Euro-dollar market in particular contributed towards bringing about a decline of the dollar's supremacy.

This in spite of its contribution to the prestige effect of the increased adoption of the dollar as the leading international currency. That prestige effect was liable to be offset by the psychological effect of the outsize sword of Damocles that was hanging over the dollar in the form of the ever-increasing volume of Euro-dollars. If the dollar had remained as strong as it was twenty years earlier the existence of a gigantic Euro-dollar market would have been a source of additional strength. But since it became inherently weak the Euro-dollar market tended, on balance, to weaken it further. It was part of the tragedy of the dollar that its extended use and its increased prestige became one of the main causes of its crisis.

CHAPTER SEVEN

The Approach of the Climax

WHATEVER advantages the achievement of the dollar's supremacy brought to the United States, she had to put up with the disadvantages and risks that went with them. These risks and disadvantages are all too familiar to those who have been following the heated controversy over sterling's role as an international currency waged ever since Britain's return to the gold standard in 1925. There are some incontestable advantages attached to that role for the benefit of the country whose currency plays it – the 'reserve currency country' as it is now called – in the form of invisible earnings and trade benefits, not to speak of national prestige which means financial, economic and political power. The question that is subject to controversy is whether the price paid for these advantages is not apt to be too high.

By the late '60s the dollar's victory over sterling was complete. Had that victory been achieved twenty years earlier the disadvantages attached to the dollar's quasi-monopolistic position in the international monetary sphere might have been negligible. The technical and psychological position of the dollar was then so strong that it could have faced any additional pressures arising from its international functions with the same degree of equanimity as sterling faced them during the nineteenth century.

In the meantime, however, the basic position of the dollar became much weaker, and it became incomparably more vulnerable. One of the reasons for the change was the development and expansion of the Euro-dollar system described in the last chapter. The inverted pyramid of the international paper-credit structure became much more precarious and the maintenance of its equilibrium became much more precarious. Realising the increased need for reinforcing the defences of the dollar to enable it to fulfil its increased international responsibilities – in addition to the burdens of the Vietnam War etc. – the Johnson Administration and the Nixon Administration adopted some deflationary measures. As we saw in the last chapter, they were only partly effective, owing to their circumvention through wholesale American borrowing in the Euro-dollar market. Even so, the resulting business recession and the increase in unemployment stepped up political pressure to induce the Government to reverse the unpopular policy.

In order to improve the chances of winning the election of November 1972, President Nixon took steps to increase consumer demand. A series of measures was adopted to that end early in 1971. His tame economic advisers managed to give him exactly the advice he wanted to receive. They elaborated a convenient economic theory according to which it would be possible for the United States to spend itself out of wage and price inflation by stimulating the increase of the output through increasing consumer purchasing power and consumer demand. Had it not been for the spreading of the 'English disease', the new policy might have produced some results, but even then only at the cost of aggravating the inflationary pressure on the dollar. But by 1971 American trade unions became almost as greedy and short-sightedly selfish as their British counterparts had been for many years. Wages were increasing at a much faster rate than production. From time to time there were some major strikes paralysing a high proportion of American industry.

For the sake of reinforcing the dollar against the effects of overseas military expenditure, but also owing to the growing unpopularity of the Vietnam War in the United States, it was decided to escalate the reduction of American armed forces in South-Eastern Asia. The result was an increase of unemployment through the demobilisation of tens of thousands of men and through the reduction of arms production. This increased further political and social pressure in favour of reflation.

Accordingly, Mr Nixon followed in 1971 Mr Heath's bad example by reducing taxation in the middle of runaway wage inflation. Inevitably the resulting increase in consumer demand reinforced the bargaining power of trade unions and stepped up wage inflation. The pseudo-theoretical basis for this inexcusable blunder was the assumption that an increase in the output in order to meet the increased consumer demand would reduce the cost of production per unit and would therefore enable producers to cut their prices. This is incontestably true in a stable, well-balanced economy. But amidst self-aggravating wage inflation any cost-reductions that would be achieved through an increase in the output are unlikely to offset the additional costs of higher wages resulting from the reinforcement of the trade unions' bargaining position that is caused by the increase of the output through stimulating consumer demand.

Nor is the excuse given for tax cuts, that the effect of the increase in private spending would be offset by cuts in public expenditure, very convincing. It would have been astonishing if the cuts in expenditure announced by Mr Nixon on 15 August 1971 had even checked the net increase of total public spending, although they slow down the rate of their increase. In any case this defence of Mr Nixon's policy was in flagrant contradiction with its main objective, to stimulate consumption. Assuming, for the sake of argument, that his cuts in public expenditure would really offset the loss of revenue resulting from lower taxation, there would then be no increase in total consumer demand. Mr Nixon and his advisers really should not try to have it both ways.

The trouble was that the American economy, like the British economy, got into an impasse. Inflation and deflation were running concurrently. Any attempt to strengthen the dollar by means of deflation was bound to aggravate the recession, while any effort to mitigate the recession was bound to increase wage inflation. After an effort to deflate in 1970, during 1971 Mr Nixon and his new Secretary of the Treasury, Mr Connally, adopted a definitely reflationary policy by relaxing the credit squeeze in order to ensure that by the time of the election in

November 1972 unemployment should become materially reduced. Yet they must have been fully aware that this result could only be achieved at the cost of weakening the international position of the dollar.

This policy was inconsistent with the oft-declared determination of the United States Government to maintain the dollar at its gold parity of $35. The overvaluation of the dollar, which was one of the main causes of the gigantic balance of payments deficit in 1970, was deliberately increased in 1971 by adopting policies that were fated to lead to further wage increases and price increases.

In an effort to escape the consequences of its self-contradictory policy the Washington Administration stepped up its pressure on Germany, Japan and other countries to induce them to revalue their currencies, so as to obviate the necessity for the United States to devalue the dollar or to deflate in order to correct the overvaluation of the dollar. As a success of those efforts came to be widely anticipated by the spring of 1971, there was a landslide-like flight from dollars to the Deutschemark and other currencies.

All this aggravated the pressure on the dollar. For speculators, merchants or investors it mattered little whether the parities of the dollar with these currencies would be brought about by a devaluation of the dollar or by an revaluation or upward floating of these other currencies, so long as these appeared a likelihood of an increase in the value of the Deutschemark in terms of dollars.

Precisely because the dollar had become the all-important international currency, buying pressure on revaluation-prone currencies assumed the form of selling dollars. In addition to sales arising from longer leads and lags on trade between the United States and the countries concerned, leads and lags on trade between third countries invoiced or financed in terms of dollars also increased the pressure on the dollar. In the old days it was mainly sterling that suffered through such international leads and lags, but now that the dollar assumed the part formerly played by sterling the burden fell on the dollar.

If Australian wool exported to Japan was invoiced or financed in dollars the Australian exporters sold the dollars forward as soon as the contract was signed. Japanese importers on their part left it to the last moment to cover their dollar requirements, in the hope that in the meantime the exchange rate would change in their favour. They increased their lags on their imports invoiced or financed in dollars not only to safeguard themselves against the risk of a devaluation of the dollar (which would have reduced the Japanese yen prices of wool imported from Australia) but also to safeguard themselves against an identical effect of a revaluation of the yen.

Hedging on foreign investments in the United States also increased selling pressure on the dollar as and when it was becoming more and more obvious that the exchange rates based on the $35 gold parity were becoming untenable. Until comparatively recently American investors in Britain were usually hedging against a devaluation of sterling by selling forward the value of their investments, whether they consisted of sterling securities or direct investments in UK industries. But by early 1971 the dollar came to be regarded as being distinctly weaker even than sterling, so that American investors removed the hedges or allowed them to expire. All this reduced the demand for dollars.

Conversely, non-resident investors in the United States came to deem it imperative to safeguard themselves against a depreciation of the dollar which was expected to occur almost any time. It is true, UK investors were prevented from doing so through the absurd inconsistency of the British exchange control regulations under which non-resident investors in Britain were permitted to hedge against a devaluation of sterling but British residents investing abroad were forbidden to hedge against a devaluation of other currencies, since they had no contractual claim maturing on a definite date. But such perverse application of exchange control was largely confined to Britain, and non-residents in most other countries with investments in the United States were at liberty to sell dollars forward to safeguard their investments against the consequences of a devaluation of the dollar or a revaluation of their own currencies. This was actually done on a large scale.

The official American policy, aiming at a drastic reduction of interest rates from the fantastically high level they reached in the late '60s, resulted in additional pressure on the dollar through re-hoarding of gold. Since gold hoarding is financed largely with the aid of borrowed Euro-dollars the rise in interest rates had made prolonged gold hoarding very costly, so that most hoarders and speculators deemed it advisable to take their profits or to cut their losses when they came to realise that an increase in the official American price of gold was not imminent. Hence the decline in the free market price of gold to the level of the American official price. When, however, Euro-dollar rates and other interest rates declined considerably there was once more a revival of gold hoarding and speculative buying of gold. The rise in the market price of gold to well over $40 reinforced the wave of pessimism about the future of the dollar.

On top of everything else, pure speculation in the form of buying Deutschemarks or other revaluation-prone currencies against dollars assumed considerable dimensions. Such speculation was done to a large extent in the London foreign exchange market which, being the largest market in dollars, provided ample facilities for speculators. In theory such operations in London were supposed to be restricted by the maximum limits on long or short position which the Bank of England permitted any London bank to have. In practice, however, the limits applied to *net* positions, so that there was nothing to prevent foreign speculators from buying in London hundreds of millions of Deutschemarks so long as they bought them against dollars and not against sterling.

In his statement in August 1971 President Nixon blamed foreign speculators for the difficulties of the dollar. What he said was true, but it contained only a relatively small part of the truth. It seems highly probable that the pressure on dollars due to the lengthening of leads and lags, hedging on investments, re-hoarding of gold and withdrawals of foreign short-term or long-term capital invested in the United States was until the last week that preceded the suspension many times larger than speculation in the narrow sense of the term. Over and above all, there was also an outflow of American capital on an increasing scale. Even after the reinforcement of official and unofficial exchange control, there was a wide variety of opportunities for United States residents to transfer their capital abroad, in addition to smuggling dollar notes to Canada.

It was not until the imminence of some drastic action became quite obvious that speculators in the narrower sense of the term stepped up their operations, the volume of which then attained spectacular dimensions. This was what happened in respect of sterling during the week that preceded its devaluation in November 1967, when Mr Callaghan's unwillingness to repeat once more his oft-repeated promise not to devalue sterling let loose an avalanche of speculative selling. Likewise, the absence of yet another repetition of the reassuring official statements by the Washington Administration about the dollar during the second week of August triggered off a flood of selling, a high proportion of which was purely speculative. When a change of parities or a suspension of parities comes to be considered imminent it would be little short of a miracle if a great many speculators did not try to grab a profit from it.

An explanation is not an excuse, however. There could be no justification for speculators to exploit the situation for the sake of speculative gains. In any case, while Mr Nixon rightly condemned speculators who were trying to make a profit through attacking the dollar, he was less vocal in condemning those of his fellow-citizens who added to the difficulties of their country by taking advantage of one or the other of the loopholes for transferring their capital abroad. Yet they were even more blameworthy than foreign speculators who owed no loyalty to the United States.

Anyhow, it is open to question whether Mr Nixon and other official American spokesmen had any moral right to condemn those who sought to avoid a loss arising from the effect on the dollar of the ill-advised policies adopted by his administration. The blame must be placed fairly and squarely on the

shoulders of those who embarked on reflation in 1971 instead
of doing their utmost to reinforce the dollar, regardless of the
short-term effect of measures required to that end.

By the spring of 1971 it became obvious that the pressure on
the dollar was becoming unbearable, and that something was
bound to break. The publication of the annual report of the
Bank of International Settlement in June 1971, which disclosed
the full extent of the expansion in the volume of Euro-dollars,
gave the market fresh food for thought. The shock given by the
official confirmation of the full extent of the increase might have
been mitigated by the publication of the BIS statistics in more
frequent intervals. As it was, the announcement of the full
extent of America's external short-term liabilities in the form of
Euro-dollar deposits must have contributed in no slight degree
towards aggravating the prevailing pessimism about the situation and prospects of the dollar.

There was some degree of relief when in May 1971 Western
Germany allowed the Deutschemark to float upward. But her
example was only followed by the Netherlands and there were
two minor revaluations. These and the appreciation of the
floating exchanges were far from sufficient to restore equilibrium
to American price levels and to enable the United States even to
reduce the trade deficit, let alone eliminate it. Moreover, whenever parities are changed or abandoned even by one single
country or by a small number of countries, this inevitably
weakens the faith of the market and of the business world in the
maintenance of the remaining fixed parities, or even in the
maintenance of the recently changed parities at their new level.

The abandonment of the old parities by four nations led to
the anticipation of further steps in the same sense by other
nations. Nor was it taken for granted that the appreciation of
the Deutschemark that followed the suspension of its stability
had gone far enough to restore the American balance of payments. Therefore the flight from the dollar into Deutschemarks
continued.

Most Central Banks became increasingly reluctant to absorb
more dollars. So long as the Bretton Woods system remained in

force they felt impelled to do so, because the alternative would have been to allow the dollar to depreciate in terms of their own currencies, which was inadmissible under the rules of the IMF. A number of Central Banks insisted on converting part of their newly acquired dollars into gold and the Federal Reserve met some of the demands. It was becoming increasingly obvious, however, that if more Central Banks insisted on their rights the United States would have to suspend convertibility. Some of the Governments came under political pressure to refrain from insisting on their rights. They were said to have been allowed to be understood that their demands might force the United States to reduce the American armed forces overseas.

Notwithstanding such pressure, the situation was obviously becoming untenable. The United States Government was expected at any moment to decide to devalue the dollar or to allow it to float. Nothing short of water-tight exchange controls similar to those adopted during the war would have been able to maintain the dollar much longer at its $35 parity.

The crisis came to a climax during the second week of August, largely as a result of the publication of a Report by the Subcommittee on International Exchanges and Payments of the Congressional Joint Economic Committee. It emphatically stated that 'a decrease in the external value of the dollar, at least against several major currencies, is required to rectify the US balance of payments'. It recommended that, in the absence of an adequate realignment of parities through the IMF, 'the United States may have no choice but to take unilateral action to go off gold and establish new dollar parities'.

One of the reasons why the findings of the Congressional Subcommittee created a profound impression at home and abroad was that until comparatively recently its chairman, Representative Henry Reuss, was one of the firmest defender of the policy to maintain the dollar at its old parity at all costs. The fact that even he now found it necessary to abandon the old parity showed that it was no longer politically impossible for the Government to act, in the hope that its action would be endorsed by Congress. Consequently, the widespread anticipation of an early action came to be intensified. As a result the sales of dollars during the second week of August assumed dimensions comparable with the sales of sterling in November 1967 on the eve of its impending devaluation.

It became impossible for Mr Nixon to defer drastic action any longer. Accordingly he announced on 15 August a batch of measures, the most important of which was the suspension of the convertibility of the dollar. Since the dollar had been already virtually inconvertible this did not make much difference in practice. What was much more painful to other countries was the imposition of a 10 per cent surcharge on all import duties and the extension of the application of the 'buy American' rule to a number of additional imports. This was done partly in order to secure a bargaining weapon with the aid of which Mr Nixon hoped to obtain trade concessions, but mainly in order to force the leading industrial countries to revalue their currencies, so as to obviate the necessity for the United States to devalue the dollar.

It was for the sake of maintaining the gold parity of $35 that Mr Nixon adopted measures liable to create a currency chaos leading to a world slump, and to split the free world into two hostile camps. Right up to December 1971 the idea of a devaluation of the dollar was looked upon as anathema in American official circles.

CHAPTER EIGHT

Why not Devalue the Dollar?

BY 1971 the dollar's position was becoming quite obviously untenable. There was growing realisation within and outside the United States that it was grossly overvalued and that 'something was bound to break' in the near future. Uncertainty about the form that the approaching climax would assume when it was reached handicapped investment to some measure throughout the free world. Yet the long-overdue decision to do something would have been deferred even longer if Mr Nixon's hand had not been forced by the publication of the Reuss Report. Even though the recommendations of his Joint Congressional Sub-committee in favour of suspending the convertibility of the dollar and abandoning the parity of 1934 were not altogether unanimous, they had the immense authority of Congress behind them. The response of the markets to those recommendations left no choice for Mr Nixon, who was no longer in a position to argue that Congress would oppose a departure from the gold parity of $35.

The difficult situation could and should have been relieved with the proverbial stroke of the pen, through a devaluation of the dollar. Until the end of 1967 I was strongly opposed to that solution. But the devaluation of sterling and the ensuing flight from dollars into gold forced me to come to the conclusion that the deterioration of the international monetary situation had proceeded too far to be reversed by means of deflation. For the extent of deflation required in order to bring about the necessary readjustment would have to be so high that it might have triggered off self-aggravating business recession degenerating into slump. The world might have experienced a return of the mass unemployment of the '30s, with the difference that this time the millions of unemployed might not have submitted meekly to their fate. During the late '60s there was a world-wide deterioration of discipline and a wave of violent demonstrations. Mass unemployment would have greatly aggravated the difficulty of maintaining law and order.

Devaluations of individual overvalued currencies and revaluations of individual undervalued currencies merely provided temporary solutions of the problems of individual countries, largely at the expense of other countries. What was called for was an all-round readjustment of parities, to be initiated by a substantial increase in the official American price of gold. But the United States Government was firmly opposed to the idea, as firmly as it had been opposed up to March 1968 to the idea of abandoning the support of the free market price of gold. The Washington Administration was not only against a 'maxi-devaluation' but also against a 'mini-devaluation' that would have corrected the overvaluation of the dollar for the time being, without solving its basic problem. Yet the chronic selling pressure which kept the dollar most of the time at its minimum support points in relation to the strong currencies made it obvious that a devaluation was called for.

Why this unwillingness of America to abandon the parity of $35? By 1971 the weight of argument was overwhelmingly in favour of a devaluation, even though expert opinion disagreed about its extent and about the form it should assume. It is an attitude that may best be compared with the British attitude after the First World War – the determination to restore sterling's pre-war gold parity and to maintain it regardless of the disadvantages of an overvalued currency. The psychology of that attitude was at any rate understandable if not acceptable. The gold parity of sterling was, ever since the adoption of the gold standard in 1816, 84s. 10½d. per ounce of fine gold. The operation of that parity coincided with the century during which Great Britain was the most powerful, the most prosperous and the most expanding Empire since Ancient Rome. Abandonment of that parity would have been regarded as being equivalent to abandoning all hopes that the British nation would ever recover its former position as the world's leading nation.

There may be a similar psychological explanation of the equally absurd American determination to retain the parity of the dollar at $35 per ounce of gold. Admittedly, it was not the original gold parity, which was $20.19. It was the rate to which the dollar was devalued in 1934 as a result of a series of crises. There was no reason for Americans to be proud of the parity of $35. But its adoption was followed by a gradual recovery from the gravest economic crisis into which the United States was ever plunged, and since the adoption of that parity the formerly frequent cyclic crises have not recurred. There have been recessions but no slumps. This was not because of any magic quality of the $35 parity. To begin with, it was because of rearmament and war in Europe, war economy in the United States from 1941, and the application of the Bretton Woods system of stability, combined with Keynesian counter-cyclical monetary policy, since the war. Americans should have sentimental attachment for economic reasons to the Bretton Woods system and not to the parity of $35. Yet the abandonment of Bretton Woods was decided in August 1971 for the sake of being able to maintain – in theory at any rate – the $35 parity. But we must remember that the operation of that parity happens to coincide with the period of American national greatness, as the existence of the original sterling parity coincided with British national greatness.

For the sake of maintaining that parity the United States Administration allowed interest rates and unemployment to rise to crisis level during the late '60s even in the absence of an acute economic crisis. For well over a decade the dollar remained more often than not at its minimum support point in relation to various currencies. Although that period was punctuated by frequent sterling crises and occasional crises of other major currencies which created diversions for the benefit of the dollar, the dollar could only be maintained at its parity at the cost of declining gold reserves and increasing external short-term indebtedness.

Of course it has become a tradition amongst leading countries not to devalue in cold blood. No matter how overwhelming the case for devaluation may have been, their Governments would not resort to it unless and until the crisis assumed such dimensions as to make further resistance impossible. This was what happened with sterling in 1931, in 1949 and in 1967, and with the dollar in 1933, when it had to be allowed to depreciate to the level at which its new parity was fixed in 1934. The only outstanding exception was the deliberate, unnecessary and useless devaluation of sterling at the outbreak of the Second World War.

Although pressure on the dollar was escalating in the late '60s and at the beginning of the '70s, it did not become irresistible until the late summer of 1971. Confronted with sales of dollars running into hundreds of millions day after day, and with the growing reluctance of Central Banks to absorb those sales, the United States Government decided to abandon the parity. It did have the choice between adopting drastic exchange controls, fixing another parity and allowing the dollar to float. It took the latter course, presumably for the sake of upholding the unconvincing fiction that the parity remained at $35 and the deviation of the actual exchange rate was purely temporary.

There are admittedly precedents for such financial make-believe. During the First World War sterling was supposed to remain convertible into gold, but most people who tried to insist on their right to exchange their Bank of England notes for sovereigns were somehow 'dissuaded' from doing so. Immense importance was attached to upholding that fiction. The recent publication of a memorandum drafted by Keynes, in his capacity of economic adviser to the Treasury in 1917, disclosed that both he and his chief, the Chancellor of the Exchequer, Reginald McKenna, firmly believed at the time that Britain would be unable to continue to fight Germany if she allowed herself to become discredited by abandoning the fictitious convertibility of sterling.

Within a few years both Keynes and McKenna became determined opponents to the monetary use of gold. But thanks to the publication of the collected works of Keynes, they are now on record, in Vol. XVI, containing Keynes's papers during the First World War, as having been extremist supporters of the gold standard only a few years before they came to predict the reduction of gold to the role of scrap metal.

At the time when these two prominent experts opposed the termination of the fiction of sterling's convertibility on the ground that it was vitally important to uphold it, they were behaving as Mr Nixon and Mr Connally did until 15 August 1971. For the convertibility of the dollar into gold was also largely fictitious years before it was officially suspended – a fact which was candidly confirmed in the Reuss Report. It is true, in exceptional circumstances some relatively small dollar holdings of Central Banks were converted into gold recently. All that happened on 15 August was that the virtually complete unofficial inconvertibility of the dollar became official and universal. Nevertheless the meaningless parity of $35 was maintained.

The question is, would it not have been wiser if, instead of 'suspending' the convertibility of the dollar, the Government had devalued it, retaining its convertibility at a realistic parity. The answer to this question depends largely on whether one believes in the all-curing effects of floating exchanges or not. All those in favour of that system welcomed Mr Nixon's decision with enthusiasm and considered it a decisive victory for their persistent campaign. Opponents of floating exchanges hoped that the floating period would prove to be merely a brief transitional stage that preceded eventual devaluation. There was something to be said for the view that it became politically easier for Mr Nixon to devalue the dollar after its *de facto* depreciation during its floating period. But many of us believed that Mr Nixon was doing the right thing for the wrong reason and in the wrong way.

By 1971 it ceased to be politically impossible for the Administration to devalue the dollar. Its inevitability came to be widely realised, and so was the urgency of solving the deadlock. There is reason to believe that Mr Nixon would not have encountered any great resistance to devaluation by Congress. Of course it would have been impossible to introduce previous legislation to that effect, as it would have taken months, or at any rate weeks, before both Houses of Congress passed it, and meanwhile speculators would have played havoc with the dollar. But it would have been practicable to carry out a *de facto* devaluation by raising the price at which the Treasury would be prepared to sell gold to foreign Central Banks. There could be no doubt that Congress would have confirmed the change once accomplished. The argument in favour of allowing the dollar to float as a necessary preliminary stage that must precede devaluation for political reasons is therefore invalid, and the suspension of convertibility in preference to immediate devaluation was decided upon for the wrong reason.

Moreover, the method chosen for it was wrong. What the American economy needed was not a moderate downward floating of the dollar, the extent of which was largely determined by foreign Central Banks, not even a mini-devaluation which, combined with the mini-revaluations of other currencies, confined the adjustment of the dollar in December 1971 to the indispensable minimum. What was needed was a 'maxi-devaluation' of the dollar, which, in addition to correcting its overvaluation, would have solved the problem of the excessive external indebtedness of the United States by reducing the gold value of her external liabilities. On the basis of the parity of $35 official dollar balances alone were three times the amount of gold holdings. Allowing for unofficial dollar holdings, the external short-term liabilities of the United States were by August 1971 five times the gold reserve. This state of affairs greatly reduced the financial power of the United States. It could and should have been corrected by a substantial rise of the official American price of gold.

In addition to the writing up of the book value of the gold reserves, such a move would have been followed by wholesale de-hoarding of gold in private possession. This was what happened after the devaluation of the dollar in 1934 and it would happen again on a much larger scale after a more substantial devaluation now. Most of the de-hoarded gold would find its way back to the vaults of Fort Knox.

Owing to the world-wide speculative short positions in dollars the covering of these short positions would have led to a substantial demand for dollars after devaluation. This would have further reinforced the financial defences of the United States.

The favourite argument against such a major devaluation was that it would be followed by an all-round devaluation which might leave the dollar just as overvalued as it is at present. But surely there is no reason to assume that such an all-round devaluation would not take into account the extent to which the dollar was overvalued in relation to the various principal currencies prior to its devaluation. After all, if the worse came to the worse there would be nothing to prevent the United States from engaging in a competitive devaluation race, as there was nothing to prevent her and other countries from engaging in a competitive depreciation race under the system of floating exchanges. Nobody would stand to gain by it, and the realisation of this fact would make it possible to negotiate an agreed set of parities. It would be much easier to persuade surplus countries to keep down the extent of their devaluations than to increase the extent of their revaluations just to suit the convenience of the United States.

In a number of quarters the unpegging of the dollar and other major currencies was welcomed not as a means for adjusting fixed parities but as a gesture indicating America's willingness to abandon the system of fixed parities. Having suffered much inconvenience in recent years through excessive rigidity of fixed parities, advocating the opposite extreme – the adoption of excessive elasticities – has become fashionable in the United States. Advocates of floating exchanges prefer freely fluctuating exchanges to occasional adjustments of fixed parities to their ever-changing equilibrium levels.

Another argument against the change of the dollar's gold parity and in favour of the suspension of the parity was that the American authorities had no means of estimating the level at which equilibrium could be achieved, and they would devalue too much or too little. Hence the preference for a floating dollar which, they believed, would float to the right level.

A frequently used argument against a major devaluation of the dollar is that it would open the floodgates for inflation. Beyond doubt a major devaluation resulting in undervaluation would make it easier to expand credit without being penalised by a decline of the reserve below danger level. But the degree of inflation does not depend on the potential limits of credit expansion. When the United States possessed $25 billion gold reserve there was no inflation comparable to the inflation that prevailed after the decline of the reserve to $10 billion.

The truth of the matter is that, unless a more reasonable spirit is introduced among workers, wage inflation will continue to prevail and the resulting increased credit requirements will be satisfied somehow. Now that the dollar is no longer convertible the extent of potential credit expansion is no longer limited by balance of payments considerations, and the Federal Reserve is no longer deterred from inflation by fears of withdrawals of gold. But the difference is more apparent than real. The limitations to credit expansion by the Bretton Woods system were not really effective. Only the form of credit expansion was much less sound than it would have been if it had been based on an increase of the gold reserve. The inventiveness of human genius produced a wide variety of methods by which credit could be expanded – increased IMF drawing rights, SDRs, reciprocal swap facilities, Euro-currency markets, parallel money markets of various kinds, etc. All these devices increase the volume of unsecured non-self-liquidating paper credits. They make the inverted pyramids of the credit structure less stable. A substantial devaluation would have strengthened the gold basis of that pyramid. The abandonment of stability further increased the possibilities of inflating with impunity. These considerations have been disregarded by the United States when deciding in favour of floating exchanges in preference to a major devaluation.

It would have been wise if this system had been adopted merely as a transition period to precede devaluation. But it appeared unsafe to take this absolutely for granted. There was no indication whatever that this was the intention of the Nixon administration. Their attitude was made deliberately obscure at the London Conference of Finance Ministers at the end of August 1971, and at the Washington meeting of the IMF in September, when Mr Connally refused to consider a substantial devaluation of the dollar as distinct from some minor temporary depreciation of the actual exchange rate. And he was blowing hot and cold at subsequent negotiations, until Mr Nixon came to commit the United States to devaluation.

The sheer absurdity of the American attitude in preferring to restore the balance of payments by means of protectionist measures rather than by means of a straightforward devaluation is equalled by the strange attitude of the other nine Governments represented at the London meeting in demanding that the balance of payments should be put right by a devaluation of the dollar and the surcharge should be dropped. For the surcharge tends to eliminate the deficit exclusively through reducing American imports. So far from contributing to the restoration of the equilibrium by increasing American exports, it actually tends to reduce them, because the existence of a protected and expanded domestic market reduces exportable surpluses and weakens the incentive for export drives. It also tends to make American goods less competitive abroad by raising their costs and their prices.

From an American point of view it would be a more efficient way to balance the deficit by making American goods more competitive both at home and abroad as a result of an adequate devaluation of the dollar. Conversely, from the point of view of the other industrial nations it would have been preferable if equilibrium had been aimed at by means of the surcharge rather than by means of a devaluation of the dollar. For while as a result of the surcharge American goods became more competitive at home they become less competitive abroad. This meant that the industrial nations stood a chance to derive compensation for the loss of their American domestic market by capturing some of the market for American goods outside the United States.

That they preferred a solution which was to their disadvantage while the United States prefers a solution which was to her disadvantage read like a passage from *Alice in Wonderland*. Fortunately by December 1971 common sense came to prevail. The Washington agreement of the Finance Minister of the Group of Ten, providing for a realignment of parities, was based on the recognition of the axiom that prosperity and stability, like security, are indivisible. The new system of parities was the result of much give-and-take on the part of all Governments concerned.

Credit is due to the United States Government for making the concessions which made an understanding possible. Having been used to playing the role of the free world's financial dictator, it could not be easy for her to realise the need for negotiating with other Governments on a more or less equal footing. Had it not been for Mr Nixon's eleventh-hour willingness to co-operate in the realignment of parities and at the same time to abandon his protectionist measures, the world might be by now in an economic turmoil and the united front of the free countries might have been ruined beyond repair.

CHAPTER NINE

'Everybody Else Is Out Of Step'

IN 1971 the dollar rate was at its minimum support points most of the time in relation to several currencies, and the Central Banks of the countries concerned had to buy up hundreds of millions of dollars week after week to prevent its depreciation. The financial assistance which most Western European countries and Japan had received from the United States on an unprecedented generous scale came to be reciprocated by these countries by their willingness to buy virtually inconvertible devaluation-prone dollars and to abstain from insisting on the conversion of their dollars into gold. Even the Bank of France, having converted under the de Gaulle regime most of its dollars into gold, was prepared to hold the dollars obtained through France's current influx of dollars. Both the Bundesbank and the Bank of Japan accumulated, very much against their wish, very large dollar reserves. This in spite of the certainty that they would suffer eventually a loss on their holdings, either as a result of a depreciation or devaluation of the dollar or as a result of an appreciation or a revaluation of their own currencies. The increase of the Bank of England's reserve assumed largely the form of dollar holdings.

The United States Government, while embarking on reflation that was doomed to destroy the last chances of defending the dollar, reaffirmed again and again its pledge to maintain its gold parity. But quite evidently it had not the least intention of embarking on the dangerous degree of deflation that would be required in order to enable it to carry out its pledge. Miracles seldom occur in the twentieth century. And it would have taken a miracle, given the policies pursued by the United States, if the persistent pressure on the dollar had come to an end without a devaluation of the dollar or an all-round revaluation of all important currencies in terms of dollars.

Of course it might have been practicable to maintain the stability of the overvalued dollar in spite of the reflationary measures in the same way as Germany did in the '30s with the aid of drastic exchange controls. While Britain, the United States and most other countries abandoned the gold standard in the early '30s and allowed their exchanges to float, Germany maintained the stability of the Reichsmark through introducing almost watertight restrictions, discontinuing free dealings in foreign exchanges. Even though during the '60s the United States departed to some degree from the principle of free international transfer of money; the extent of restrictions and 'guidelines' was moderate. By and large, dealing in foreign exchanges was left reasonably free. It would have been contrary to the principles and basic philosophy of the Washington Administration to solve the dollar problem by means of adopting watertight exchange control.

An alternative to defending the overvalued dollar behind a wall of exchange controls was its defence by means of trade barriers. Even though the measures announced by Mr Nixon on 15 August included a 10 per cent surcharge and other protectionist measures, it would be gross exaggeration to maintain that the United States adopted the policy of defending the dollar by economic isolationism even remotely comparable with the systems adopted by a number of countries in the '30s. While the surcharge was useful as a supplementary measure to the other measures and as a bargaining weapon for bringing pressure to bear on Japan and on Germany to revalue their currencies, in itself it would not have been sufficient to balance the American deficit in face of escalating inflation.

Another alternative was to reduce the overvaluation of the dollar through the adoption of a drastic incomes policy. Mr Nixon's measures did in fact take a step in that direction by decreeing a pay freeze and price freeze for three months, after the end of which period an incomes policy and a restraint on prices and dividends would come into operation. But it seemed doubtful whether Mr Nixon would be prepared to go far enough in implementing a policy if it were found to unpopular, for the sake of reducing the degree of the overvaluation of the dollar. In any case, since the policy of increasing consumer demand in order to reduce unemployment continued to be pursued, the outlook for a successful incomes policy appeared to be anything but promising.

In the circumstances the only way in which it would have been possible for the United States to maintain the dollar parity at $35 was a revaluation or upward floating of the leading currencies, especially the Deutschemark. For the sake of checking the wholesale influx of unwanted dollars West Germany and the Netherlands did go some way towards meeting the wishes of the United States. After an interval, Britain, Japan and other countries followed that lead. They did so reluctantly, feeling as they did that since the disequilibrium was the result of the inability or unwillingness of the United States to adopt sound policies, it should be the responsibility of the United States to correct the resulting disequilibrium by devaluing the dollar.

The reluctance of Japan and other countries to revalue to a sufficient extent to restore the equilibrium of the dollar, and the inadequacy of their appreciation, caused much resentment in the United States. The Americans were right in recalling the immense sacrifices made by the United States since 1945 to assist in the economic reconstruction and military defence of the free world. Their demand that all countries of the free world should contribute their due share to the cost of their defences by American forces was unanswerable. Indeed, it would be possible to make out a reasonable case for applying that principle in retrospect by a drastic devaluation of the dollar, which would inflict considerable losses on the two principal beneficiaries from the deterioration of the American balance of payments – Japan and Germany. This would have been very rough justice, because other countries, which also kept down their expenditure on national defence thanks to the strength of the United States – albeit not to the same extent as Germany and Japan – but which did not accumulate nearly as large dollar reserves as Germany and Japan, would not have been affected to a proportionate extent by the retrospective application of the principle. Anyhow, the United States preferred to solve the dollar problem in a different way – by inducing the countries of the free world to revalue or float their currencies upward to such an extent as to mitigate the extent of correcting the overvaluation of the dollar by means of its official devaluation.

Beyond doubt, the free world owes a very great debt of gratitude to the United States. She saved Western Europe in two World Wars, and she assisted in the economic reconstruction of victims and vanquished alike. By assuming the role of the supreme defender of the free world after the Second World War she protected both allies and uncommitted nations from Russian and Chinese Communist imperialism, thereby enabling free countries to raise their standards of living instead of devoting a much higher proportion of their incomes to military expenditure. Having regard to this, it is the moral duty of the countries of Western Europe and of Japan to go out of their way to assist the United States when it is the latter that requires financial assistance and when they are able to afford to assist her. It is their moral duty to meet any reasonable requirements of the United States. It is also to their vital interests to do everything in their power to help the United States to recover her financial strength sufficiently to be able to continue to play the leading part as the supreme defender of the free world.

To give an instance of my interpretation of our duty to assist America in safeguarding her genuine interests, when in the spring of 1971 Rolls-Royce got into difficulties and it endangered the continued existence of Lockheed, whose salvage was absolutely vital to the defences of the United States, I published a letter in *The Times* demanding that the British Government should rescue Rolls-Royce regardless of costs. I argued that even if this should cost Britain hundreds of millions of pounds, it would amount to a bare fraction of the many billions of aid received by this country from the United States since 1914.

It is the moral duty of all free countries to meet any reasonable requirements of the United States if it is within their means to meet them. The accent is, however, on 'reasonable'. It was reasonable on the part of the United States to expect Britain to help to salvage Rolls-Royce. It was reasonable on the part of the Washington Administration to expect the Common Market to abstain from adopting measures of discrimination in trade that would be gravely detrimental to American agriculture and industry. It was reasonable to expect the free world to put up with American protectionist measures without retaliation, since those measures were essential to enable the United States to restore her balance of payments. After all, if the deficit running at an annual rate without precedent in time of peace continued at such a rate the United States would be doomed. But it was *not* reasonable for the United States to expect Western European countries or Japan to adapt their national monetary policies to the requirements of the United States merely because out of sheer vanity and false pride she chose to refuse to work out her own salvation by means of a devaluation of the dollar. It was *not* reasonable to expect a number of countries to revalue their currencies, or to allow them to float upward, merely to spare the United States the necessity to devalue the dollar.

If it were really a matter of vital interests for the United States to avoid devaluation it would have been a different matter. But no vital national interests were involved in maintaining the nominal parity of $35. Quite on the contrary, it was in accordance with the vital interests of the United States to solver her problem by a drastic devaluation of the dollar. Her unwillingness to change its parity was nothing more than a matter of unwarranted pride and silly vanity. No country was under any moral obligation whatsoever to alter its monetary system or its parities merely for the sake of conforming to this unreasonable and unintelligent American attitude.

Having wasted the substance of the strength of the dollar, the United States was determined to preserve the shadow. Ten years ago, and perhaps even five years ago, the dollar was still a symbol of American world power. It would then have been the

duty of nations depending on that world power for their freedom to make any reasonable sacrifice for the sake of maintaining that symbol in all its glory. But by 1971 there remained no
glory to uphold as far as the dollar was concerned. An almost
uninterrupted series of balance of payments deficits, with no
effort either to balance them or at any rate to consolidate the
resulting external short-term indebtedness; an orgy of Euro-
dollar borrowing by American banks; the *de facto* limitation of
the dollar's convertibility into gold for official holders, coupled
with pressure on them to acquire more virtually inconvertible
dollars with the sky as the limit; all this and much else utterly
discredited the dollar. It ceased to command respect in the
world.

Why should any country have inflicted on itself loss and
inconvenience by revaluing its currency or giving up stability
for the sake of enabling the Washington Administration to keep
up false appearances which deceived nobody? Why should any
country have deemed its duty to make sacrifices for the sake of
sparing Mr Nixon the necessity of adopting unpopular measures on the eve of the Presidential election in order to save the
dollar from devaluation, merely because he chose to attach so
much importance to face-saving considerations?

'Can't you humour us on this matter?' an American acquain-
tance asked me after I developed to him the above argument.
This remark implied admission that no vital American interests
were at stake, merely a perverse puerile preference for maintaining the parity of $35. The whole agitation in favour of upsetting
the Bretton Woods system came from the unwillingness of the
United States to recognise the fact that she was the odd person
who imagined herself in step while she considered everybody
else to be out of step.

The deterioration of the dollar created a situation by 1971 in
which some countries found themselves forced to the conclusion
that even revaluation of their currencies or abandonment of
their parities were smaller evils than the unlimited influx of unwanted doomed dollars. This was why they revalued or adopted the system of floating exchanges, in most instances much

against their better judgment. When Mr Nixon announced
to the world that the dollar, too, would henceforth be floating, a
number of additional countries – including Japan and Britain –
suspended the stability of their currencies. They did this not
because they allowed themselves to be convinced that it was
the better system or that it was really necessary even from an
American point of view, but because, with the dollar and the
Deutschemark floating, the exchanges were doomed in any
case to be subject to wide fluctuations.

The appreciation of various exchanges resulting from their
revaluation or upward floating was not the result of any realisation by the Governments concerned that, since these currencies
were undervalued against the dollar, it was their duty to correct
the disequilibrium by revaluation or by upward floating. It
was sheer sophistry to quote the authors of the Bretton Woods
Agreement as the originators of a monetary system under which
it was the duty of any country whose exchange is undervalued
to take steps to restore balance. That argument would have
been valid if the dollar had been overvalued in relation to one
currency only – say, the yen – in which case balance could have
been restored by a revaluation of the yen. But since the dollar
was overvalued in relation to most currencies the Bretton Woods
spirit called for its devaluation and not for a revaluation of all
other currencies.

This basic truth was not recognised adequately even in
December 1971 when after much delay and hard bargaining
a compromise was reached. For, even though the dollar was
devalued, the extent of its devaluation was a mere 8 per cent,
not nearly enough to correct its overvaluation. A number of
other countries had to revalue their currencies to correct the
disequilibrium created by American policies.

CHAPTER TEN

'Dollar-Imperialism'

IT cannot be emphasised sufficiently or repeated often enough that it was the duty as well as in the vital interests of the Governments of the free world to do anything reasonable to assist the United States in her effort to restore the dollar's strength. But their moral obligations to that end were mitigated by the extent to which the dollar problem was her own fault. Quite obviously the countries of Western Europe and Japan could not reasonably be expected to make sacrifices and inflict near-masochistic inconveniences on themselves just in order to spare the United States of the political effects of pre-election devaluation of the dollar or to enable Mr Nixon to win the support of the American electorate by inflating with comparative impunity. Nor were the Governments of the free countries under any moral obligation to help the United States against the effects of 'dollar-imperialism' on her gold reserve.

The term 'dollar-imperialism' was first invented soon after the end of the Second World War, at a time when there was absolutely no justification for its use. Indeed the United States was giving away dollars with both hands to all and sundry, to allies and to uncommited nations, with no political strings attached to the loans or gifts. The recipients were even permitted to spit at the hand that fed them, before during and after feeding. As we pointed out in Chapter 4 Marshall aid – rightly described by Churchill as the most unsordid act in history – was only one of the various forms in which the United States enabled countries of the five continents to share in the wealth and prosperity of the world's richest and most powerful nation.

Even the potential enemy, the Soviet Union, benefited by American generosity. Its war debt owed to the United States for the gigantic war-time deliveries of arms and other goods, amounting to billions of dollars, without which Germany would have defeated Russia, was wiped out. Needless to say, the Soviet Union did not ever thank her for this magnanimous gesture. Its 'gratitude' manifested itself not only in its imperialistic designs of world conquest but also in the invention of the invective 'dollar-imperialism' which became during the '40s a byword in the Communist propaganda campaigns all over the world. It became a favourite term of abuse directed by Communists and fellow-travellers against the most generous nation in world history. It was used widely by people whose countries had derived immense benefit from American magnanimity.

The accusation of 'dollar-imperialism' was also made by de Gaulle's France, and with even less justification. It is true, de Gaulle justifiably resented the wholesale acquisition of French and other continental industries by American capital. More will be said about this subject presently. But even if France had a real grievance in this respect, she ought to have realised that military invasion would be infinitely worse than 'economic invasion', and that France owed her immunity from Russian aggression to the military power of the United States. He ought to have remembered that the United States liberated France from enemy occupation twice within a generation, and that after the Second World War she received very generous American assistance, helping her to complete her reconstruction, to stabilise the franc eventually, and to regain her economic strength and prosperity. Remembering all this, the hostile measures adopted by France to resist 'dollar imperialism' by converting the dollar reserves of the Bank of France into gold and by trying to incite other Central Banks to do likewise must be condemned as unworthy of the great idealist French nation.

I trust I shall not be suspected of harbouring unfriendly feelings towards the United States for criticising the way in which she tried in more recent years to live up to the bad name given to her by her enemies at a time when there was absolutely no justification for it. As already indicated in the Preface of this book, the criticism of the United States which I felt impelled to make about various ill-advised American policies was the criticism of a candid but sincere friend. I criticise not for the sake of being censorious, but because my denunciation of 'dollar-imperialism' provides the basis for a constructive suggestion put forward in the next chapter.

Beyond doubt, to take advantage of the over-valuation of the dollar for acquiring foreign industries on a large scale at what were by American standards bargain prices, partly for the sake of being able to employ cheaper labour, constituted 'dollar imperialism'. Some countries welcomed this invasion of American capital, as it suited the purpose of the Governments of the day. For instance the influx of American capital was received with open arms by the British Labour Government of 1964-70, because it offset much of the current balance of payments deficit. For the sake of acquiring dollars by such means Mr Wilson's Government permitted and even encouraged American big business to acquire virtual control of important British firms and even the bulk of entire industries. He and his successor who also favoured American industrial penetration failed to realise that, while at the moment of the influx of American capital it was a source of strength for sterling, its presence here was a permanent source of weakness – an ever-present threat hanging over sterling. For whenever sterling was under a cloud, American firms with direct investment in Britain were selling sterling forward in order to hedge against a devaluation. During the '60s it became quite an understood thing that wholesale selling of sterling by 'the Great West Road' (the district where factories of many American subsidiaries are situated) was one of the symptoms of sterling crises.

I wonder if de Gaulle realised how right he was from an economic point of view, in wanting to discourage the influx of American capital. He was, however, right for the wrong reason – because of a chip on his shoulder owing to resentment of his treatment by Roosevelt during the war. And he was hopelessly wrong in choosing the ways in which he endeavoured to discourage it. The right method would have been the one pursued by Japan, which country simply placed a straight ban on the

influx of American capital – a device which is within the rights
of every sovereign state. Even the Japanese method caused
strong resentment in the United States, although it was entirely
in accordance with basic American national interests, especially
in the short run. In the long run American firms and the United
States as a whole hoped to benefit by this form of 'dollar-
imperialism' through earning large profits because of the lower
wages paid abroad, and through obtaining capital gains on
direct investments abroad. In the short run, however, over-
exporting of capital accentuated the drain on the American
gold reserve. It is true, from the middle '60s the United States
adopted the practice of financing the acquisition of foreign
industries largely by borrowing in the countries concerned. To
that extent 'dollar-imperialism' no longer led to additional
losses of gold. In a negative sense, however, it produced a
similar effect, because the use of America's capacity to borrow
abroad for the purpose of mopping up dollars held abroad
would have enabled the United States to keep down the increasing excess of foreign dollar balance over the gold reserve.
Instead of strengthening the dollar by such means, American
borrowing in the Euro-bond market and elsewhere served the
purposes of 'dollar-imperialism'.

The United States did not really stand to benefit by the
excessive export of capital even in the long run. The industries
established by American capital abroad now compete with
domestic American industries. Although repatriated profits of
these firms constitute an important invisible export item, their
success has greatly contributed to the increase of unemployment in the United States. The American current balance of
payments benefits only by the profits of the subsidiaries, and
only by that part of the profits which is repatriated. But the
resulting loss of markets for home-produced goods is a burden
on the American balance of payments.

Even if the repatriated profits exceed the immediate effect of
capital exports on the American gold reserve, the United States
could ill afford to use up a large proportion of her declining
gold reserve for the sake of the distant prospect of recovering

the gold thus lost. The immediate effect of over-exporting capital contributed towards the need for the adoption of measures to defend the dollar against selling pressure, and this was highly detrimental from the point of view of the productive capacity and standard of living of the United States. It was largely responsible for the low rate of growth. Moreover, as already pointed out, the weakening of the dollar meant a decline of American power in the sphere of international politics as well as in that of international finance.

Nor did the countries which were recipients of the exported American capital benefit by it, generally speaking, on balance. A great deal has been said about the benefit derived through the acquisition of American knowhow. But Japan has evidently been doing very well even without acquiring American know-how through admitting American capital. Her industrial re-volution was second to none, and her spectacular technical advancement in recent years put many older industrial coun-tries to shame. American firms in Britain and in other countries may have been more efficient in many ways than their British rivals ·– especially technologically and in methods of sales promotion – but their labour relations were notoriously un-satisfactory. Fords had a fantastic number of strikes. The un-willingness of some American firms to apply voluntary wage restraint in Britain was an act of flagrant disloyalty and one of the causes why that policy became a dismal failure.

Having regard to all this, it is no wonder de Gaulle was op-posed to the influx of American capital. But he and his successor, M. Pompidou, ought to have opposed it in a different way. The way in which they reacted, apart from measures aiming at weakening the dollar, was to conclude a treaty of friendship with the Soviet Government and to leave NATO. Indeed, one of the effects of 'dollar-imperialism' was that French hostility to the United States converted the Common Market virtually into an anti-American alliance aiming at the defence of Europe against American industrial invasion instead of against Russian military invasion.

In more recent years 'dollar-imperialism' also manifested

itself in the American expectation that it was the duty of every country of the free world to accept and hold indefinitely un-limited amounts of virtually inconvertible inflated dollars as a matter of course, to meet the perennial balance of payments deficits of the United States, regardless of the causes of those deficits. It came to be assumed in Washington that the United States had a right to inflate the dollar to an unlimited extent, and that it was the duty of every country of the free world to correct the resulting disequilibrium between the price levels in the United States and their countries by revaluing their exchanges, or by inflating their own currencies to an extent necessary for restoring equilibrium. According to American official opinion, expert opinion and public opinion, whenever the dollar became overvalued because of the excess of American inflation over inflation in other countries it should be the duty of all these other countries to correct the resulting disequilibrium. This aspect of the subject was already discussed earlier, when dealing with American expectations of European revaluations.

Admittedly the Bretton Woods agreement did lay down the principle that disequilibrium between price levels of member countries should be eliminated, both through the measures by countries with overvalued currencies and by those of countries with undervalued currencies. But surely it was not the intention of the authors of the plan to give irresponsible governments a free hand to inflate to their hearts' desire, leaving it to respon-sible governments to adjust the resulting disequilibrium by embarking on deliberate inflation, or alternatively by revaluing their exchanges. The American conception to that effect that developed during the '60s was a gross distortion of the Bretton Woods principle.

This strange American attitude was based on the doctrine that, since under the Bretton Woods system the dollar was the centre of the monetary universe, other countries had to adapt their currencies to the dollar in all circumstances as a matter of course. What was particularly strange about this attitude was that it only emerged long after the dollar ceased to be the strong-est currency and a suitable basis of the world's monetay system.

Its strength, having reached this highest point in the middle '50s, declined almost without interruption in the late '50s and in the '60s. As we saw in earlier chapters, from time to time there were dollar scares, and several currencies came to be considered to be much stronger than the dollar. These were unpalatable facts, but they were facts all the same. They were a matter for regret to all of us who value the maintenance of the freedom of the free world, freedom which depended very largely on the maintenance of the strength of the United States, which again depended not only on her military power but also on the strength of the dollar.

This was one of the reasons why the United States felt justified in expecting the free world to bolster up the dollar. Her attitude was justified to the extent to which the declining strength of the dollar was the result of the excessive share of the free man's burden which the United States bore ever since the war and still bears. All other countries of the free world were, and still are, guilty of having kept down their defence strength, on the comfortable assumption that the United States would shield them against the imperialist-Communist menace, enabling them thereby to have a good time by spending the amounts which they saved on their own defences. To the extent to which the decline in the strength of the dollar was due to the disproportionately heavy share borne by the United States of the cost of defending the free world, she has every moral and political right to expect the rest of the free world to support the dollar by accepting and holding large and increasing dollar reserves.

If the rest of us are not happy about this attitude of the United States in expecting us to assist her financially, the remedy lies in our own hands. All we have to do is to relieve the United States of a reasonable share of the free man's burden by strengthening our own military power. Alternatively we could buy more American goods or sell less to the United States, so as to reduce her balance of payments deficit. Thanks to such changes the strength of the dollar would probably recover.

The countries of the Common Market took exactly the opposite course. By differentiating against imports from the

United States compared with imports against each other, they made it even more difficult for the United States to finance her excessive share of the free man's burden. They had only themselves to blame for the development of a spirit of protectionism in the United States.

The almost single-handed American defence of the free world by conducting a costly war in Vietnam and by maintaining military bases abroad was by no means the only cause of the weakening of the dollar. We saw above that 'dollar-imperialism' in the form of acquiring industries abroad on a gigantic scale contributed to a considerable extent to the decline of the gold reserve. To the extent to which the dollar's difficulties were due to this cause the United States had no moral claim on the rest of the free world for supporting the dollar by acquiring and maintaining unlimited amounts of it, or by deflating or revaluing their currencies. The United States would of course be fully entitled to invest in foreign industries any genuine export surplus, in the same way as Britain had invested her export surplus throughout the nineteenth century. But to run up a gigantic short-term debt abroad for the sake of acquiring the control of key industries of European countries was a totally different story. The Bank of France and other Central Banks could hardly be blamed for their unwillingness to finance such 'dollar-imeprialism' by holding the dollars spent on the acquisition of industries in their countries very much against their wish.

In spite of her heavy military expenditure abroad the United States could have retained much of her gold reserve, if it had not been for over-exporting capital. For the sake of retaining her financial strength and the prestige of the dollar this process should have been checked and reversed many years ago.

Yet strange as it may sound, short-sighted politicians and economists in the United States consider the acquisition of control over foreign industries as a source of economic and political strength. They fail to realise the extent of anti-American feeling created abroad, not only in countries like France (the Governments of which are opposed to the influx of

American capital), but even in countries like Britain, where the
Governments – Socialist or Tory alike – welcome that influx.
The reason why labour relations of American firms in Britain
are even worse than those of British firms is not only that
American managements, both of the parent firms and of the
affiliates, are unfamiliar with British labour conditions, but also
because workers employed by American factories in Britain hate
their employers, not only because they are employers but also
because they are foreign. In any case it is bad psychology to
imagine that by acquiring control of vital industries in Britain
and in other countries the United States secures the friendship of the public in those countries. Quite on the contrary,
each mismanaged wage dispute in American-controlled firms
strengthens the anti-American feeling, and so does their refusal
to co-operate in the voluntary wage restraint.

Another political aspect of 'dollar imperialism' is that, by
investing large amounts of capital in countries where Communism has already a strong foothold, the Americans gave
hostages to fortune. It is very tempting for Frenchmen and
Italians to vote into office a Government which would national-
ise American enterprise. This might occur, not only if the Communist parties of these countries gained control, but also if a
Leftish Government assumed office with Communist support.
Many Frenchmen and Italians might be tempted to vote Communist at general elections for the sake of that consideration
alone. By over-investing in Europe the United States strengthened there the trend towards Communism.

In spite of all this – and partly because of it – it was the duty
of the countries of the free world to help to save the United
States from the worst consequences of her own short-sighted
policy. One of the ways to that end was for their Central Banks
to comply with the American demand that they should continue
accepting and holding dollars in spite of the virtual certainty
that sooner or later they were bound to suffer a heavy loss on
their dollar reserves as a result of a revaluation of their own
currencies or of a devaluation or depreciation of the dollar. But
this attitude was against the true interests of the American

nation, because in doing so, the Central Banks concerned reluctantly assisted the United States Government over a long period in its unreasonable policy of maintaining the dollar at an overvalued level. It should have been obvious that this state of affairs could not possibly continue for ever. Yet month after month Central Banks continued to accept dollars derived from the current balance of payment surpluses of their countries on their trade with the United States and from the flight of funds from the United States to their countries. Even the Bank of France, which some years earlier converted its dollars into gold, was willing in 1970–1 to accumulate the current surplus in the form of dollars, although it converted into gold a substantial amount for the purpose of making a payment in gold to the IMF.

It is open to argument whether it would not have been wiser on the part of one of the large holders of dollars to bring matters to a head much earlier by insisting on its claim that its dollars should be converted into gold, in the full expectation that the United States would have to refuse to do so. Alternatively Central Banks could have stopped supporting the dollar at its minimum support point, as a result of which the dollar would have depreciated. Such action might have compelled the United States to face the realities of the situation earlier, and to abandon the old parity. In all probability even then the United States Government would have preferred to choose the solution of maintaining in theory the gold parity of $35 and adopting in practice the system of floating dollars instead of resorting to straightforward devaluation. But the period of suspense would have been brought to an end earlier and the amount of dollars piled up by most Central Banks would have been smaller.

The pride in the maintenance of the $35 parity was utterly false. By 1971 Americans had no more cause to be proud of their dollar than Britons had cause to be proud of their sterling by 1967. Both currencies were at one time symbols of national strength, national character, national integrity, thanks to which Britons and Americans had good cause for considering themselves superior and for expecting to be considered superior by other nations. But sterling and the dollar have ceased to be

symbols of British and American national greatness. Britons
have long realised this as far as sterling is concerned, and it was
high time Americans should realise that they had more reason
to be ashamed of their bankrupt discredited dollar than to be
proud of it. They had every reason to be proud of their superior
armed forces, of the superior strength of their national economy,
of their technological and business efficiency, of their unprecedented generosity, and of a great many other things. But they
were pastmasters of self-deception if they really believed that
they were justified in taking pride in the dollar as it was in 1971,
although they maintained the fiction of its old gold parity. It
would take a supreme national effort to ensure that the dollar is
respected once more. The United States Government and the
American people have yet to realise this fact.

Other nations pretending to acknowledge the non-existent
superiority of the dollar by allowing themselves to be persuaded
that it was their duty to consider the $35 parity sacrosant
probably imagined they rendered a service to the United States
Government in office. But in reality they rendered a disservice
to the American nation by delaying the moment when its
Government felt impelled to face facts and to act in accordance with the realities of the situation. By believing, or pretending to believe, that the dollar still reigned supreme, Mr
Nixon and Mr Connally deceived themselves and mislead their
nation into believing that they were justified in abstaining
from the adoption of policies which would restore the genuine
supremacy of the dollar.

With the adoption of the floating dollar on 15 August 1971,
the nominal maintenance of the parity at $35 became an utterly
meaningless outward symbol of 'dollar-imperialism'. And the
enunciation of the Nixon Doctrine that it was for foreign
Governments to adapt their gold parities to the situations
created by American monetary policy, coming as it did
simultaneously with the removal of the last vestige of the link
between gold and the dollar, was singularly ill-timed.

CHAPTER ELEVEN

The Case for Disinvestment

THE last chapter was devoted to the denunciation of over-investment abroad as one of the causes of the deterioration of the dollar. Although the argument in favour of restoring the strength of the dollar with a stroke of the pen through its drastic devaluation was sound, it would have been wishful thinking to assess very highly the chances of an adoption of this solution. Nothing short of a major disaster is likely to drive the United States into a sufficiently drastic devaluation, of an extent which would greatly exceed the immediate requirements of restoring the balance of payments equilibrium.

There is, however, an alternative device which would enable the United States to restore at least some of the strength of the dollar by increasing her reserves. This end could be achieved to a very high degree through reversing the process of excessive investment abroad. It would not be enough merely to call a halt to new net long-term investment abroad until a succession of export surpluses has wiped out the external short-term liabilities of the United States and has created a substantial amount of liquid reserves. The process would take many years. It should be speeded up by a policy of large-scale disinvestment.

It would be absurd exaggeration to contend that 'dollar-imperialism' in the form of excessive long-term investment abroad was the only cause of the deplorable decline of the external financial strength of the United States. But it is beyond doubt that over-investment did contribute to that deplorable result to a very considerable extent. If it had not been for the insatiable appetite of United States business concerns for acquiring the control and full ownership of industries in other industrial countries, and if the Government had called a halt to this export of capital in good time, the dollar would have remained a strong and reasonably secure currency. The amount of gold in Fort Knox would be still impressive and the financial power and prestige of the United States would still stand reasonably high.

In Chapter 10 we saw the obvious disadvantages of over-investment abroad from an American point of view. Even if the balance of payments of the United States had a perennial surplus – as it had in earlier post-war years – it would have been more in accordance with general American interests if American firms had been restrained by their Government or had practised more self-restraint in their zeal to acquire foreign enterprise. They ought to have pursued a more selective policy in their expansion abroad. Since in the absence of a surplus on the American balance of payments the resources genuinely available for reinvestment abroad were limited to the amounts they were able to borrow abroad, they ought to have confined themselves largely to the establishment or acquisition of firms providing for the distribution of their goods and for the maintenance and servicing of those goods. Instead, American firms, with the full approval of their Government, threw themselves whole-heartedly into a crusade of industrial world conquest. While the Soviet Union aimed at conquering the world in a political and military sense, the United States entertained similar ambitions in an industrial and financial sense.

As I tried to explain in Chapter 10, the grossly excessive acquisition of American-owned industries abroad was gravely detrimental not only from the point of view of the balance of payments of the United States but also from the point of view of the long-term interests of the American economy. Politically it was the cause of the weakening of the united defensive front of the free world against the Communist-imperialist menace, partly through the generation of anti-American feeling in Western Europe but even more through the reduction of the financial strength of the United States.

As a result of this ill-advised policy some three-fifths of the gold reserve has been replaced by illiquid industrial holdings abroad. Such holdings have also been acquired at the cost of an increase of American foreign short-term liabilities. While the United States is still the largest creditor nation on balance allowing for long-term as well as short-term assets, on short-term account alone she is heavily in the red, because of her excessive long-term investments abroad.

Of course it is always possible to put forward an ingenious theory that could be used as an excuse for mistaken and short-sighted policies. American politicians, businessmen, bankers and even economists who ought to know better put forward the argument that foreign long-term portfolio investments and direct investments abroad form just as much part of the reserves behind the dollar as gold and American liquid assets abroad. Indeed, the argument runs, while the gold stock at Fort Knox yields no return, long-term investments abroad bring in dividends and are liable to produce substantial capital appreciation. For this reason, it is argued, they are better securities for the dollar than the sterile gold reserve or low-yielding short-term assets.

What those who argue on such lines overlook is that long-term holdings lack the main quality which reserve assets must possess, i.e. liquidity. The British subsidiary of Fords may be worth a great many milions, but this asset could hardly be relied upon for meeting a run on the dollar. It was utterly ill-advised, from the point of view of the gold reserve, not to be content with holding a controlling interest in the British Ford Company and acquiring the shares originally issued and held in Britain. Long-term securities, and even direct investments, may be marketable at a price, but if holders have to realise them at short notice they might have to accept a very unfavourable price. The experience of the '30s conclusively proved that in a crisis most long-term 'reserves' are apt to become hopelessly frozen. The possession of billions in such investments failed to save sterling in 1931 or the dollar in 1933.

All this is stating the obvious. Yet the obvious truth is

flagrantly disregarded by the United States when it conflicts with business interests. Even in 1971, amidst all chronic and acute difficulties of the dollar, when the 'gold window' had to be closed, there was still additional American long-term capital invested abroad, even though on a much smaller scale than it was until some years ago. But the United States Government is still moving heaven and earth to over-persuade the Japanese Government to admit American investment.

It would not be sufficient merely to call a halt to this process. What is needed is to reverse it. During the next few years the United States should pursue a systematic policy aiming at the realisation of a substantial portion of American investments abroad. This was done by Britain in two World Wars, also after the Second World War when meat supplies from the Argentine, for instance, were paid for with the aid of British holdings of Argentine railroad stocks. The cash was needed and the advantages of holding long-term investments had to be sacrificed for the sake of meeting more important and more urgent requirements.

I am not suggesting that there should be a panicky wholesale realisation of American holdings of foreign securities. Such an operation would bring about a slump on Stock Exchanges abroad, which, in addition to inflicting losses on holders and reducing the proceeds that might be obtained for the benefit of the American reserves through a gradual sale, might trigger off crises in the countries concerned, and even a world crisis. Fortunately the realisation of the long-term assets is not all that urgent now that the convertibility of the dollar has been suspended, though it might come to be considered urgent if the selling pressure on the dollar should continue despite realignment. In the absence of adverse developments the United States could afford to take her time in gradually reducing her excessive investments abroad.

Many American holdings of foreign securities have good markets outside the United States, and their gradual realisation would not cause a slump. Indeed, it might not even check the appreciation of the stocks. An increase of the gold reserve by some billions of dollars might be sufficient for the present to reassure world opinion about the prospects of the dollar, and it would enable the American authorities to maintain the dollar at its new parity for some time, if that is the policy they should want to pursue. But it would be a mistake to confine the operation to those holdings which are easily realisable. That would leave the United States with foreign assets that could not be realised in an emergency on reasonable terms. Efforts should be made to realise some of the foreign direct investments acquired in recent years. This would also yield political benefit, as it would mitigate the resentment felt in France and in other countries over the expansion of American capital and enterprise in Europe.

It would be easy for American firms whose names are household words abroad to issue equities of their affiliates in the countries where they are established instead of issuing bonds to finance expansion. While retaining the control in American hands, local equity capital should be allowed to participate. This way of raising money is preferable to financing the affiliates with the aid of issuing Euro-bonds in the countries concerned or in other European countries. The affiliates would be much more acceptable to public opinion in the countries concerned than they are if they are entirely American owned. Sales of such participations would be particularly advisable in the case of industries in which Americans hold an excessive share, such as, for instance, the British motor industry. There would be much less talk about 'dollar-imperialism' if American capital invested in a country were more diversified and if local interests were given a chance to participate, not only as bondholders but also as investors in equities or as partners sharing the control of the firms.

The realisation of large amounts of American long-term capital would necessarily take time, which is an additional reason for getting on with the exercise before there is urgent need for doing so. The moment the sale of such assets appears to have become urgent the bargaining position of potential buyers would naturally grow stronger. Thanks to the realignment of parities in 1971, holders are in a better position to wait for the right moment and sell their assets on their own terms.

If moral suasion by the United States authorities should not be sufficient to induce holders of foreign assets to disinvest there are various means by which the Government would be able to compel them to do so. It could follow the British example in the First World War in which fiscal means were employed to induce British holders of American securities to sell their holdings to the Treasury. Or it could follow the British example in the Second World War when British holdings were simply commandeered.

Admittedly a drastic reduction of American long-term investments abroad might deprive holders and the United States as a whole of increased profits and capital gains which growth might tend to bring in due course. On the other hand, it is obviously safer to hold gold or short-term assets than it is to hold foreign equities. Possibly the long boom may have passed its peak and we might experience a relapse or a gradual decline, which would mean cuts of dividends and capital losses on foreign investments. American holders of foreign industrial stocks have not concluded a covenant with providence to the effect that growth is to continue uninterruptedly forever. Already there was in the early '70s an increase in the number of major bankruptcies in Europe, including some first-class names. Even if gains should outweigh losses in the long run – which should not be taken for granted – the higher risk is a consideration which should not be overlooked.

In any case, to reinforce the dollar and to restore the financial prestige of the United States by increasing her gold reserve and her other liquid international net assets would be an advantage that would be worth some sacrifices of profits. In addition to the economic advantage of more rapid growth at home, large-scale disinvestment abroad would place the United States once more in a position of power in the sphere of international finance, which would entail strengthening her political power. In this connection it is worth re-emphasising that large participations in foreign industries are not a source of strength. On the

contrary, by investing unduly large amounts in foreign countries, the United States would give hostages to fortune. The
control of vital industries does of course secure for American
firms influence in the countries concerned, but only so long
as the Governments of those countries attach importance to
maintaining friendly relations with the United States Government and to attracting more American capital. The larger the
amount of American investments in a country, the more power
has its Government to bring pressure to bear on the United
States. Fiscal devices, threats of nationalisation – threats which
were actually implemented in a number of countries – and
various forms of xenophobic legislation are liable to inflict
heavy losses on the American firms concerned. In given situations the foreign policy of the State Department is liable to
be influenced in a sense unfavourable to national interests for
the sake of safeguarding American sectional business interests
against hostile action.

The amount of American investments abroad should be
drastically cut not only for the sake of recovering a large part
of the gold lost as a result of these investments but also for the
sake of reducing the power of foreign Governments to damage
American business interests.

It is true, it would have been tantalising for American firms
to miss good investment opportunities abroad if they had the
necessary capital available or were in a position to raise it
in the United States, merely because of the effect of their investments on the gold reserve. But in order to be able to assess
the net profits, if any, which they will eventually derive from
the increase of their investments abroad from the point of
view of the United States as a whole, it is necessary to allow
for the effects on domestic business of credit restraint and
other measures which the Government felt impelled to adopt
to defend the dollar against pressure due to over-investment
abroad. Losses arising from those measures were incalculable,
but it does not seem unreasonable to suggest that they exceeded
considerably any likely gains to be derived from the increased
foreign investments. In any case, investment opportunities

within the United States are far from having been exhausted. Many American firms preferred to acquire affiliates abroad rather than expand their plants at home, because of the high cost of American labour. Admittedly, wages are lower in many foreign countries, but if allowance is made for the higher productivity of American labour it is doubtful whether it is always safe for American firms to allow their decisions to invest abroad be influenced by this consideration. Moreover, labour conditions in Britain for instance have been a great deal worse than in the United States, where trade unions, however greedy they may be, are at least intelligently greedy and enforce discipline among their members to prevent frequent unofficial strikes and other forms of unofficial industrial action that inflicts heavy losses on American subsidiaries in Britain, where trade unions are stupidly greedy and are in any case unable to enforce discipline among their members.

It should be remembered that so long as unemployment is high in the United States it is against the public interest for American firms to import even more unemployment by exporting capital.

Apart altogether from all these considerations, it would be worth while for the United States to forgo some genuine economic advantages for the sake of regaining her international financial power. It would not be beyond the realm of possibilities to increase the gold reserve materially by a gradual and selective realisation of a high proportion of direct investments as well as portfolio investments in foreign countries. But there are no indications that the United States Government or the American business world has realised that it was a grave mistake to over-invest abroad, and acceptance of the above unsolicited advice for reversing the process appears to be most unlikely. It would stand a chance if history should repeat itself and large-scale widespread losses such as those suffered by America abroad in the '30s should teach her once more a lesson that has been forgotten all too soon.

Last but by no means least, the United States will need at home the capital that could be raised by disinvestment abroad, for financing the adoption of anti-pollution devices. It would involve highly expensive reconstruction of industrial equipment, but it would be the best investment America has ever made. It would reduce pollution at home instead of increasing it abroad.

CHAPTER TWELVE

Some Political Considerations

THE case for and against the prolonged defence of the dollar's old parity, as the case for and against excessive export of American capital, must not be judged solely on the basis of economic considerations. Grave political considerations were also involved, and to my mind some of them were even more important, indeed much more important, than the sum total of economic considerations. The latter concern the prosperity and economic stability of the United States and the other countries of the free world. The former concern the maintenance of their freedom. Important as it is to maintain our progress towards a higher standard of living and to avoid taking undue risks of relapsing into chaotic economic conditions, it is infinitely more important that the people of the free world should be able to retain their freedom in face of the menace of enslavement by Communist-imperialists.

Of course, in a sense, economic progress and stability assist the free world in the defence of its freedom, apart from other reasons because a comparison of the standard of living on both sides of the Iron Curtain goes some way towards discrediting Communist propaganda. But too much weight should not be attached to this point. To judge by the high proportion of Communists in France and in Italy, standard of living is not the only consideration – *pace* Karl Marx – that determines the politics of people. Anyhow, it will be seen later that high priority given to high standard of living is liable to be detrimental to national security.

In this chapter we are not concerned with the indirect effects of the prolonged overvaluation of the dollar on the chances of Communist imperialism to achieve their ends as a result of an absolute or relative economic deterioration in the free world. What we are concerned with here is its direct politico-military effects.

By weakening her financial power, the United States has greatly reduced her capacity to defend herself and the free world against enslavement by imperialist-Communist dictatorship. Surely this consideration must transcend any consideration of standard of living. The United States jeopardised her security and that of the free world by continuing to defend the $35 parity long after it became obviously indefensible, in addition to making it more indefensible by an *excessive* increase in the standard of living, and by over-exporting capital.

Britain has sacrificed her national greatness for the sake of adopting an over-generous welfare state and for the sake of achieving full employment regardless of the facts that those who benefit by them did not show the best appreciation of their benefits. The United States is well on her way towards sacrificing her national greatness for the sake of much less idealistic ends – the widespread ambition of Americans to acquire the latest model of motor car every year and for the sake of gaining control of industries in advanced countries. Owing to a high and ever-rising standard of living in the United States, even the increasingly efficient American industry was unable to produce sufficient exportable surpluses at competitive prices to cover the balance of payments deficit arising from high overseas military expenditure and from excessive capital exports. High standard of living was largely responsible for the high costs of the overseas military expenditure. An army encumbered with showerbaths, ice-cream-making machines, cinemas, etc., is bound to be at a disadvantage against an army the requirements of which are kept at bare subsistence level and which can live on the country where it is fighting. High domestic demand in the United States due to ever-increasing standard of living ensured a vast home market that obviated the necessity for most firms to go out of their way to secure overseas markets.

To revert to the instance of motor cars referred to above, were is not for the ridiculous American automobile-snobbery, because of which anyone who drives last year's model of a car is looked upon as if he would be wearing a week-old shirt, the United States would have exported many more cars and she would have imported much fewer cars.

In Britain the adverse balance of payments was a major political issue. Its deterioration was partly responsible for the defeat of the Labour Government in 1951 and for the defeat of the Conservative Government in 1964. In the United States foreign trade constitutes such an insignificant percentage of the national income that its ups and downs play only a marginal part, if any, in influencing election results. Mr Nixon is mistaken in assuming that parities or exchange rates are liable to influence the American electorate. When he suspended the convertibility of the dollar and the dollar started floating downward it hardly caused a ripple on the American political horizon. American public opinion was much more concerned with the 10 per cent surcharge, and with other protectionist measures, which were welcomed with enthusiasm, and with the pay freeze and price freeze which had a mixed reception. Compared with the effects his measures are expected to produce on wages, prices, dividends, domestic trade and employment, his measures affecting the external value of the dollar are most unlikely to produce any noteworthy political influence.

From this point of view, it will make no difference if the depreciation of the dollar had been caused, not by 'closing the gold window' leading to a depreciation, but by an immediate devaluation through a reduction of the official selling price of gold. Now that it occurred at long last, no American will lose any sleep at the thought of a change in the gold parity, which, having regard to the fact that the dollar has been inconvertible for domestic holders ever since 1933, means absolutely nothing to at least 99.9 per cent of the American public.

It is well to recall in this connection that within a month from the suspension of the gold standard in Britain in 1931 the National Government responsible for the decision won the general election with a record majority.

Mr Nixon's pre-election reflation early in 1971 was utterly

ill-timed from the point of view of its likely effect on the election result. In the absence of his measures of August 1971 the first batch of measures would have produced their effect too soon, and by November 1972 their long-term adverse effect would have ruined Mr Nixon's chances. On the other hand, his second batch of measures, into which he was forced willy-nilly by the unpopularity of his Administration due to high unemployment, stands a good chance of creating a boom just in time to secure victory – since reactions to those measures abroad were prevented by the concessions made in December 1971. He is much more likely to lose the election as a result of his courage and honesty in adopting an incomes policy and restraining price and dividend increases.

So much for the domestic political aspects of devaluation or depreciation. Their international political effects are infinitely more important from the point of view of the free world, and even from the point of view of the United States. It seems reasonable to assume that the militant attitude of Communist countries was greatly encouraged during the concluding years of the '60s and the opening years of the '70s by their knowledge that the United States had every intention of weakening its financial power through defending the parity of $35 instead of safeguarding her financial strength for the task of containing Communist-imperialist aggrandisement. In 1931 it was the succession of crises in Britain and in the United States that encouraged Japan to invade Manchuria, on the correct assumption that both powers were too preoccupied with their domestic economic troubles to take a firm line against her enterprise. There is good reason to believe that the reason why Soviet Russia stepped up the execution of her world-conquering plans in the Middle East and in the Indian Ocean, and why North Vietnam was encouraged from Moscow and Peking to persevere with its war of aggression instead of concluding a negotiated peace with the United States, was the assumption that the United States could ill afford to continue to resist her aggression, since her first and foremost aim was to defend the dollar at its gold parity.

Opponents of a devaluation of the dollar frequently argued, and not without effect on American political and public opinion, that an increase in the American price of gold must be avoided because it would benefit the Soviet Union in its capacity as the world's second largest, possibly largest, gold producer. This argument is puerile. The adult way of looking at it is that a devaluation of the dollar is either beneficial for the United States or it is damaging, and that if it is beneficial it is sheer nonsense to refrain from it merely because Soviet Russia also stands to gain by it. Moreover, any financial gain of the Soviet Union obtained through being able to sell gold at higher prices is certain to be offset by the favourable effect of dollar devaluation on the capacity of the United States to restore a balanced economy, and to resist communist-imperialist aggression. For the sake of defending the parity of the dollar the United States relinquished or weakened her role as the principal defender of the free world. Soviet Russia stood to benefit by this policy to an incomparably higher degree than the financial benefit derived from a higher price of gold.

Nobody would think of opposing the invention of a cure for cancer on the ground that sufferers in potential enemy countries would also benefit by it.

One is permitted to wonder to what extent the decision to speed up the withdrawal of American Forces from South Vietnam was due to balance of payments considerations rather than to mounting political pressure on the Government. It may be worth recalling that the reason why the French Government did not resist the Nazi re-militarisation of the Rhineland in March 1936 was the fear that the expenses of a display of force through a partial mobilisation would have weakened the franc further. The franc had to be devalued just the same in September 1936, and it was for the sake of deferring its long-overdue devaluation by six months that the French Government of the day sacrificed France's national security. History has the bad habit of repeating itself, because its lessons are not heeded by nations not directly concerned.

It was largely because of the self-imposed handicap of the United States by defending her gold parity that during recent years Soviet Russia was able to penetrate the Middle East and the Indian Ocean. The hawks in the Kremlin assumed correctly that the United States, being gravely preoccupied with the defence of the dollar, could not afford to take the necessary steps that would have neutralised the change in the balance of power in favour of imperialist-Communists.

It is the long-term ambition of the Soviet Government to gain supremacy over India and/or over Western Europe before China becomes sufficiently industrialised and militarised to upset the balance of power in favour of Peking. The next few years will be therefore a critical period for the free world. So long as the United States remains preoccupied with the defences of the dollar instead of concentrating on the containment of Soviet Russian expansion she might fight with one of her hands tied. When Mr Nixon used that analogy in justification of his measures he was evidently oblivious of the fact that it was he himself and his predecessors in office who tied one of the hands of the United States by giving top priority to the maintenance of the $35 parity. But from this point of view the difference between defending the dollar at parities determined by the gold price of $35 or at its new parity of $38 which might be overvalued and might become subject to selling pressure is a mere matter of degree.

The mini-devaluation of the dollar to $38 might not make a fundamental difference from this point of view. Indeed inadequate devaluation is liable to lead to anticipation of further instalments on the assumptions that only the first step was difficult. Having abandoned Bretton Woods parities, the Washington Administration further weakened general confidence in its determination to hold the dollar at a definite level, unless the dollar becomes undervalued and reserves for its defence are plentiful. Pressure on the dollar is liable to increase after inadequate alignment of the parities, and once more it might become necessary to concentrate increasing efforts on its defence. Even if the realignment appeared at the moment tolerable, the dollar is liable to become overvalued once more in the absence of a national regeneration.

CHAPTER THIRTEEN

Devaluation or Revaluations?

THE question whether the correction of the dollar's overvaluation should assume the form of its devaluation or of the revaluation of a number of important currencies was the subject of heated controversy. Official American opinion, backed by the 'dollar lobby' and by many American academic economists, was fanatically opposed to a major dollar devaluation, on the ground that since the dollar was the basis of the world's monetary system its gold value must be considered sacrosanct and it was the duty of every other country to adapt its parities in a sense as to ensure the equilibrium of the dollar. Under the Bretton Woods system a change in the gold parity of the dollar would mean 'an all-round change of all parities, which would leave the dollar overvalued'. This nonsense, and the refusal to realise that the dollar has ceased to be strong enough to remain the basis of the world monetary system, was and still is the main obstacle to a sensible solution of the dollar problem. Yet from the moment when the United States ceased to convert official holdings of dollars freely – to be exact, when she began to 'dissuade' the holder from insisting on conversion – the dollar ceased to play the role allotted to it by the rules of the IMF.

But Americans were not alone in advocating the revaluation of other currencies in preference to a devaluation of the dollar. On the assumption that a major devaluation of the dollar would remove the last obstacle to advanced international inflation, the idea that parity readjustments should assume preferably the form of a revaluation of other currencies instead of a devaluation of the dollar, found support in some anti-inflationist quarters outside the United States.

This controversy may be regarded as a new version of the age-old conflict between inflationists and deflationists. But it should not be assumed that all anti-inflationists are necessarily revaluationists and that all devaluationists are necessarily inflationists. I for one am in favour of a dollar devaluation, not because of its inflationary implications but because I am convinced that devaluations or revaluations would make little difference to the world-wide inflationary trend.

During the last quarter of the nineteenth century the controversy assumed the form of bimetallism *v.* monometallism. Most inflationists favoured the retention of the monetary use of silver for the sake of ensuring the expansion of the volume of monetary metals, or at any rate for the sake of preventing its drastic reduction as a result of the demonetisation of silver which was proceeding fast. After the decisive victory of the gold standard, expansionism assumed the form of advocating a managed gold standard and a gold exchange standard which came to be widely adopted between the wars. Not content with the resulting expansion, extremists such as the social credit school were in favour of the determination of the volume of credit independently of the volume of monetary gold, on the basis of social requirements which are limitless. They received strong if qualified support even from respectable experts such as Keynes and McKenna.

After the suspension of the gold standard in the '30s the conflict assumed largely the form of favouring or opposing an early return to stable parities, the alternative being the adoption of controlled paper currencies such as the Reichsmark was since 1931. It was found that in Germany it was feasible under the protective shield of exchange control, and even more under the totalitarian regime of the Nazis, to bring about a considerable degree of monetary expansion with the aid of a currency divorced from gold, thereby creating employment and financing rearmament.

During the Second World War the planned and controlled economies of the belligerent countries reduced their inconvertible paper currencies to what Arthur Greenwood called 'meaningless symbols'. Production came to be determined by the

amount of labour, materials, etc., available, and not by the
amount of credit resources which was adapted to the requirements of production. Consumption was determined by rationing.

The inflation *v.* deflation controversy was resumed after the
war in the form of a controversy between those who wanted to
perpetuate cheap money with its inflationary implications and
those favouring a return to fluctuating interest rates. The continued maintenance of cheap money until the change of Government in 1951 resulted in non-stop credit expansion. The
only means by which banks were able to meet the expanding
credit requirements was through the sale of their Government
securities accumulated during the war. The Bank of England
bought up the amounts offered in order to prevent a rise in
interest rates. This system virtually amounted to the adoption of
social credit, even though few of the supporters of that system or
their opponents appeared to have realised it.

After the advent of the Conservative Government the system
of cheap money was abandoned and during the '50s and early
'60s the system of 'stop-go' under which reflation alternated
with deflation was in operation. The controversy assumed the
form of a conflict between those favouring Keynesian counter-
cyclical policies and those preferring non-stop expansion for the
sake of everlasting economic growth at an ever-increasing pace.

The disagreement between those who regarded the IMF as a
stabilising influence with powers to enforce discipline and those
who conceived its main role as an instrument for international
expansion ended in the decisive victory of the latter, not only
through the gradual increase of quotas and drawing rights but
particularly through the adoption of SDRs – largely unconditional gifts with only limited obligations for temporary part
repayment. Under the Barber Plan even this limited obligation
would probably be removed, so that SDRs would become
unconditional gifts.

While the controversy between the opposing schools was
going on, in practice inflation was proceeding and escalating,
apart from temporary interruptions followed by additional
phases of inflation. Deflation, or even checking of inflation,

became socially more and more difficult and politically virtually impossible in most countries. Vested interest in favour of continued inflation became too strong to be resisted. In any case, paper-credit came to assume such gigantic dimensions that effective effort to bring its volume under control would have required dangerous deflationary measures. Since attempts to apply such measures would have been politically unpopular, most Governments became increasingly reluctant even to call a halt to inflation, let alone reverse it.

Even though the effect of this inflation on the cost of living and the frequently recurrent currency crises created by the difference in the degree of inflation in various countries was worrying, it was not sufficiently worrying to frighten Governments and public opinion into coming down definitely in favour of returning to deflation, or at any rate to stability at the cost of deliberately checking economic growth.

This policy of virtually non-stop inflation was attacked by France under de Gaulle, who, advised by M. Jacques Rueff, would have liked to put the clock back by doing away with the gold exchange standard and reverting to a pure gold standard. This formed the theoretical basis of the conversion of the Bank of France's dollar reserve into gold, even though, as we saw in Chapter 10, the main cause was de Gaulle's hostile feeling towards the United States. Anyhow, following on the disturbances in 1968, even France had to escalate her inflation.

In reality all academic arguments for and against inflationary or deflationary policy became irrelevant in practice as a result of the change of the balance of power in favour of the trade unions. Thanks to the high degree of employment the trade unions held most of the trumps, and thanks to the excessive welfare state benefits their bargaining power remained high even during recessions when unemployment increased. The 'English disease' which undermined industrial discipline and kept down producitvity spread from Britain over other industrial countries and became mainly responsible for the escalation of world inflation in spite of growing unemployment.

The theoretical foundations of the situation such as has

existed since the war provided what we may conveniently call the 'inverted Money School'. According to the fashionable Money School everything depends on the quantity of money. In reality the quantity of money is in existing circumstances not the cause but the effect of the increased money requirements resulting from the escalating wage inflation combined with growth-hysteria. Judging by experience of recent years, wage inflation tends to continue regardless of whether the background is inflationary or deflationary, despite high unemployment, even though there may be a difference in the rate of its escalation.

Owing to the spreading of the 'English disease' over the United States, in addition to the various circumstances described in previous chapters, the defence of the dollar at its old parity became increasingly difficult. But the United States Government was determined to correct the overvaluation of the dollar through inducing other Governments to revalue their own currencies or to allow them to float upward, in order to spare the United States of the need for effecting the readjustment by a devaluation of the dollar.

As pointed out at the beginning of this chapter, the myth was conceived that, since the dollar was the centre of the monetary universe, its gold parity was immutable. On the basis of that notion, the United States expected all countries to disorganise their economies as a matter of course, and to inflict heavy losses on themselves for the sake of obviating the necessity of changing the dollar's gold value.

Of course the American contention that since the dollar was the basis of the monetary system and the world was on a dollar standard it could not possibly be devalued became untenable because of the weakneing of the technical and fundamental defences of the dollar. Mr Nixon's irresponsible decision early in 1971 to embark on pre-election inflation disqualified the dollar from servicing as the basis of the monetary system. The dollar standard ceased to exist when it was decided to sacrifice its intrinsic value for the sake of electioneering considerations. Its use as a standard of value may best be compared with the use of a tape measure made of rubber, enabling those who use it to make it longer whenever this happens to suit their convenience.

It was of course possible to argue that amidst the turmoil of uncertainties of the world's monetary system we must have a 'fixed point' to which all other unstable magnitudes must adapt themselves, and the immutable gold parity of the dollar was supposed to provide that fixed point which must not, therefore, be interfered with. It had been argued in favour of the maintenance of that parity on the ground that it should remain the one thing stable in this world of instabilities, while other parities, exchange rates and prices kept changing. But in view of the inflationary policies of the Government which was supposed to safeguard the stability of this 'fixed' point, it ceased to qualify for acting as a 'fixed' point.

The disqualification of the dollar from being able to serve as the much-needed 'fixed' point became completed when on 15 August 1971 Mr Nixon officially suspended its convertibility into gold at a fixed price, or indeed at any price. The dollar became just one of the number of floating currencies, none of which command sufficient respect or confidence to be adequate to serve as a reserve currency. Anything might have happened to them. The fact that the American economy is the world's strongest does not, as Mr Nixon seems to imagine, mean that the dollar must necessarily be considered to be the basic currency.

Only inherent strength or some degree of scarcity qualifies a currency for being able to play the role of serving as a basis of the monetary system. What disqualifies the dollar more than anything else is the application of the 'Nixon Doctrine' which, if fully applied, would obviate the necessity for the United States Government to make any effort whatsoever to maintain or restore the inherent strength of the dollar. Mr Nixon seems to claim it as America's birthright to inflate whenever the spirit moves her Government in that sense, and to any extent convenient to her, on the assumption that when as a result the dollar gets out of equilibrium with other major currencies it is the duty of the countries to revalue their currencies to the extent required for the restoration of the dollar's international equilibrium. Unless and until Mr Nixon or his successors repudiate that thoroughly unsound doctrine by word and by action the dollar can never fill the prevailing monetary power-vacuum. The compromise of December 1971 failed to solve the problem.

On the face of it, it might be arguable that a major dollar devaluation must necessarily escalate inflation, while a revaluation of other currencies tends to produce the opposite effect. This assumption implies that by abstaining from a devaluation of the dollar thanks to the revaluation of other currencies the United States could and would avoid inflating, while the countries which revalued their currencies find themselves in a position in which they have no choice but to deflate in order to defend their currencies which became overvalued as a result of their revaluation. This assumption is false for more than one reason.

A revaluation of foreign currencies obviated the necessity for the United States to defend the dollar by adopting deflationary measures, or even by mitigating the escalation of her inflation. If the dollar is no longer devaluation-prone the American authorities feel they may inflate with impunity – that is, with impunity in the sense that they would suffer no more loss of reserves through an adverse balance of payments or through pressure resulting from a flight of capital from the dollar into some revaluation-prone currency. It would not secure immunity for the American people from punishment for its inflation in the form of a steeper rise in its cost of living. Such immunity could only be secured, or at any rate the punishment might be reduced, by reverting to the much-maligned policy of 'stop-go' in spite of a restoration of the international equilibrium of the dollar through revaluations by foreign Governments.

Repeated revaluations of other currencies whenever domestic inflation in the United States makes the dollar overvalued would obviate the necessity for the United States Government to check expansion, fully as effectively as would a repeated devaluation of the dollar. But owing to the importance of the American economy in world economy, non-stop inflation in the United States, even if accompanied by frequent revaluations of other currencies, would tend to stimulate the international inflationary trend.

So much for the all but generally accepted argument that a substitution of revaluations of other currencies for a dollar devaluation would be a move in favour of checking world inflation through checking the contribution of the United States towards it.

The argument that revaluation or upward floating of a currency necessarily entails deflation or even that it checks inflation in the country concerned is untenable. It is based on the assumption that, if a currency becomes overvalued as a result of its excessive revaluation or appreciation, it would have to be defended by deflationary measures at its overvalued level. That assumption may be correct if the revaluation is excessive and if the Government concerned prefers to defend its overvalued exchange at all costs instead of correcting the dis-equilibrium by a downward adjustment of its exchange rate. Both assumptions are essentially unrealistic. While some Governments, once they decided to revalue, may prefer to err on the safe side in order to avoid having to repeat the exercise, most Governments want to avoid excessive revaluation which would penalise their exporters. It would entail trade recession through foreign competition at home and abroad and through the application of restrictions necessitated by the deliberate overvaluation of their currencies. In practical experience since the war all revaluations and upward floatings proved to be inadequate and gave rise to expectations of another instalment or revaluation or appreciations to come. Although temporarily the covering of long positions in the revalued currency concerned caused a decline of reserves, in the long run abnormal demand for these currencies was resumed sooner or later in anticipation of a further revaluation.

This experience is liable to repeat itself, owing to the in-adequate degree of the adjustment, or to further inflation in the United States which might necessitate a repetition of the exercise if and when the dollar should become once more over-valued. In recent times, the two Anglo-Saxon nations have become basically inflationary, while Germany, Japan and France showed more determination to resist inflation. As a result, an adjustment through a revaluation of their currencies could not possibly solve the problem once and for all. Even if the extent of the revaluation of the Deutschemark and the yen were adequate for the moment, new difference between the degree of inflation in Germany and Japan on the one hand, and in Britain and the United States on the other, is liable to create a new state of disequilibrium in the course of time. Sooner or later DM and yen would become undervalued and there-fore they would become once more revaluation-prone. There would develop another sweeping flight of funds into those currencies. This actually happened to the Deutschemark which remained revaluation-prone despite its repeated upward ad-justments.

In such circumstances the revalued currencies need not be defended with the aid of deflationary measures, because antici-pation of their further revaluation would ensure their firm trend even if they allowed the influx of foreign funds to produce its inflationary effect. But revaluation is usually followed by some deflationary measures, not for the sake of defending the ex-change at an overvalued level but in order to offset the in-flationary effect of a new influx of funds in anticipation of another instalment or revaluation. The response to such mea-sures is usually an outcry which is apt to force the authorities to reverse their restrictionist policy, which does not command popular support if it is considered unnecessary because their exchanges are firm. In any case, thanks to the operation of the Euro-currency markets and of the Euro-issue markets, in some countries business firms are able to circumvent the credit squeeze by borrowing in these markets.

Since thanks to revaluations or upward floating of foreign currencies the United States is now in a better position to inflate with impunity she might step up inflation, especially in election year. In 1971 taxes were greatly reduced in spite of the fact that the resulting increase in the demand was bound to step up wage demands. Having regard to the upward trend of wages and prices, and to other reasons, it seemed probable that in practice public spending would continue to increase in all countries. As we have pointed out already, the most we are entitled reasonably to expect is that the rate of increase of public spending might be reduced. Much-publicised cuts in expenditure are offset and more than offset by increase of spending on other items. It remains to be seen whether in face of the underlying inflationary trend Mr Nixon's attempt to apply price restraint and wage restraints will succeed in 1972.

Countries which revalued and sought to deflate found that the effect of their deflationary measures was largely offset by wage inflation due to the existing balance of power between employers and employees. Revaluation might slow down the pace of inflation, but not necessarily. We are on the wage standard and, as already pointed out, the volume of money is adapted to the increased requirements resulting from the higher wages. Governments are unable or unwilling to resist the resulting demand for more money. Allowing for all this, it seems that the argument in favour of revaluations as an alternative to a devaluation of the dollar on the ground that they would check world inflation was far from convincing.

One of the main reasons why Central Banks were against revaluation is that it reduced the value of their gold and foreign exchange reserves in terms of their national currencies. It would have suited them if the disequilibrium had been offset by a dollar devaluation. This was why the proposal was adopted by the Group of Ten in December 1971, that the United States and the rest should meet somewhere halfway, by combining a minor devaluation of the dollar with moderate revaluations of other currencies. The rise in the value of their gold reserve through the higher dollar price of gold offset more or less their losses resulting from the revaluation.

This consideration is of secondary importance and should only marginally affect the attitude of countries with revaluation-prone currencies. To refuse to revalue in order to avoid losses on gold and foreign exchange reserves, if apart from this consideration there was a strong case in favour of revaluation, would have been as unjustified as to decide in favour of devaluation largely for the sake of making a profit on the official reserves. Changes of parities are of vital importance and must be decided upon solely for the sake of very important basic considerations – restoration of equilibrium between price levels, checking of self-aggravating inflationary or deflationary trends in the domestic economy, dealing with a large chronic balance of payments deficit or surplus, restoration of confidence in a currency, etc.

CHAPTER FOURTEEN

'Too Late and Too Little?'

WHEN in 1936 France abandoned the gold parity of the franc fixed eight years earlier by M. Poincaré, there followed a series of mini-devaluations and spells of depreciation. The French Finance Ministers that followed each other in close succession were all fighting desperate rearguard actions against a drastic adjustment of the franc to a level at which it would have become tenable in spite of domestic inflation. They delayed every downward adjustment until it became inevitable, and then they kept down its extent to the minimum. Each of these mini-devaluations was condemned by Paul Reynaud, the leading financial expert in French politics in the '30s and later Finance Minister and Prime Minister, as having been 'too late and too little'. That self-same verdict came to be repeated many times in many countries after the war. It will no doubt serve as the appropriate epitaph for Mr Nixon and for Mr Connally. They will go down in history as having inflicted incalculable harm on the United States and on the free world by their ill-advised policy preventing a timely and adequate adjustment of the dollar.

To give them their due, it is to their credit that they did recognise in August 1971 the inevitability of abandoning the hopeless defence of the dollar. They could not help facing the facts of the run on the dollar and of the expected refusal of several Central Banks to continue to absorb even more dollars in an effort to bolster up the rate at the minimum support point. It seemed that in a matter of days the United States would be confronted between the choice of allowing the dollar rate to float or defending the dollar by drawing extensively on the gold reserve. The closing of the 'gold window' and the adoption of the system of a floating dollar was bad enough, but Mr Nixon and Mr Connally did choose the smaller evil. It would have been even worse if they had used up the entire gold reserve, or even a large part of it, to postpone the evil day on which they had to concede defeat. The realisation of the need for doing so came very late – as we saw in Chapter 13, American losses and the Soviet Union's politico-military gains from the delay must have been incalculable – but perhaps not 'too late'. On the other hand, I would not be surprised if we found that the extent of the resulting adjustment was 'too little'.

Such credit as the United States Government was entitled to claim for conceding the principle that the exchange parities based on the gold parity of $35 were after all not sacrosanct was more or less offset by the inadequate extent and the hopelessly mistaken way in which they came to apply their new policy.

Once they abandoned the basic principle it became a matter of expediency to choose the level at which the dollar stood a good chance of becoming self-supporting without any need for sacrifices in terms of national defence. There was no justification whatsoever for trying to keep down to a minimum the devaluation of the dollar by laying down the rule that its *de jure* parity of the dollar must remain at $35 and that all other nations must adjust their gold parities to a level at which their exchange rates would suit the requirements of the United States. Mr Nixon and Mr Connally must have surely been aware that Germany, Japan and all advanced industrial countries would do their utmost to keep down to a minimum the self-inflicted handicap on their exports resulting from a revaluation or upward floating of their exchanges.

Once the rigid defence of Bretton Woods parities was given up, the United States had an opportunity to carry out a maxi-devaluation of the dollar. We saw it in earlier chapters that, as a result of the decline of the gold reserve and the increase of the external short-term indebtedness of the United States, the dollar became a highly vulnerable currency, much to the detriment of the power and prestige of the United States. What was needed was a sufficiently substantial increase of the official price of gold to raise the value of the gold reserve to a level at which the dollar would be able once more to look gold in the face.

A devaluation of the dollar to half, or preferably a quarter, of its parity of 1934 would have gone a long way towards solving not only the problem of the United States but also that of the entire free world. Instead of building up inverted pyramids of inconvertible paper-credit in various forms, a sufficiently broad gold basis would have been created for the inflated credit structure of the United States and the rest of the free world. The accumulation of near-astronomic figures representing liabilities and claims in the form of book-entries is liable to lead to a gigantic disaster sooner or later, to a financial and economic crisis of a magnitude compared with which the disasters of the '30s would disappear into insignificance. The question is only when the inevitable crisis would occur and what form it would assume.

In 1971 Mr Nixon had the power to save the free world from this nightmare. He could have created financial stability and security – not forever, of course, but for a great many years, possibly for several decades. The grossly inflated credit structure created for financing war and reconstruction and the un-precedented world-wide economic expansion since 1945 would have rested on much more solid foundations. It would have been no longer 'secured' by mere book entries which in turn are 'secured' merely by other book entries, but by gold with intrinsic value. But, like the French Finance Ministers in the late '30s, he preferred to keep down the inevitable adjustment to a minimum. He was no Roosevelt to make a bold gesture that would have created at least the preliminary conditions for the restoration of confidence in the dollar and in the capacity of the American economy to resume its accelerating expansion without being handicapped by the vulnerability of the dollar and to pursue political and military policies in accordance with the basic interest of America's security. In the course of time expanding requirements and rising prices might have made the gold basis of the credit structure once more inadequate. But possibly the lesson taught by the experience of our generation might have been heeded and the evil day when the dollar would come once more under a cloud might have been deferred for a long time.

The great disadvantage of mini-devaluations – or for that matter of mini-revaluations – is that the markets, the business world, investors, trade unions, consumers etc., expect each instalment to be followed by another and yet another instalment. Suppose for the sake of argument that after the 'mini-revaluations' and 'mini-devaluations' agreed upon by the principal countries in 1971 after a great deal of hard bargaining with much give-and-take the dollar ceased to be overvalued – for the present. Even so, there would be no means of foreseeing the extent of pre-election inflation in the United States. Possibly by the autumn of 1972 the dollar might be once more overvalued and, after a temporary recovery, there might be another recession. Mr Nixon might then administer another and yet another dose of inflation. That would necessitate additional revaluations of other currencies as an alternative to a devaluation of the dollar, which Mr Nixon would be more anxious than ever to avoid on the eve of the election.

After the experience of December 1971 official disclaimers of intentions to reduce the exchange value of the dollar commanded even less confidence than they did before August 1971. Had the dollar been devalued to a very considerable extent most people would be content to take it for granted that the operation was meant to be for his lifetime of an entire generation. But any mini-devaluations or mini-depreciations were liable to increase distrust in the stability of the dollar at its new level.

There is worse to come. By laying down the rule that it was for foreign Governments to determine the exchange value of the dollar, the President of the United States abdicated his constitutional responsibility to the people of the United States to carry out one of the most important functions of his Government – the determination of the value of the national currency. Each time leading industrial nations decide to agree that the value of the dollar is inconvenient to them they would henceforth feel entitled, under the Nixon Doctrine, to alter its value – not necessarily to suit the convenience of the United States but to suit their own convenience. It may be that the present revaluations and appreciations suit the immediate convenience of the United States. But quite conceivably under the system that is meant to replace the Bretton Woods system of stability the leading Governments might decide on the next occasion to determine the international value of the dollar which would not suit the American Government and the American nation. They might feel justified in doing so on the basis of the precedent enforced by Mr Nixon himself.

The present willingness of several Governments to help Mr Nixon up to a point by enabling him to restore temporarily the balance of payments without any unduly painful measures of deflation or major devaluation might appear to suit the immediate interests of the American people. But even if this precedent were followed up by further changes of parities or exchange rates that would be equally convenient to the United States, taking the long view it would be against her basic national interests. The consequence of being thus pampered would be a debasement of the American character, just as the consequence of Britain being pampered by a never-ending series of financial assistance in the '60s was a debasement of the British character. It would come to be taken for granted that whenever the United States gets into a mess through her own fault she would be rescued with the assistance of other Governments. The incentive to work out her own salvation would be reduced to a minimum. It would be assumed that the world owes her a living.

Even conceding the possibility that during the first six months or twelve months the system of realigned parities would operate relatively smoothly, it would be unwise to assume that it is a satisfactory alternative to genuine stability. Quite possibly nothing might happen for six months or twelve months that would make us realise the self-aggravating character of frequently repeated changes in parities. Yet the experience of

France – to mention only one of the leading countries – during the '50s and the experience of many countries between the wars and also more recently, clearly shows that repeated changes of parities make it increasingly difficult to maintain the new parities in face of buying or selling pressure.

This means that there can be no ideal or even near-ideal solution for the dilemma of choosing between excessive rigidity and excessive flexibility of parities. The disadvantages of stubborn resistance to persistent pressure due to disequilibrium are only too obvious. But if a Government gives way to such pressures in order to avoid these disadvantages the market may come to assume that it would give way too easily, which assumption would tend to stimulate pressures. The choice is between two unsatisfactory solutions.

During the years that preceded the devaluation of the dollar in December 1971 its excessive rigidity was a source of much trouble. Because the extent of its devaluation in 1971 was kept down to a minimum it might well be widely assumed that a further instalment or several instalments of devaluation are liable to follow in due course. There can be little doubt that a parity of, say, $70, or even $60 or $50 would have commanded more confidence than the new parity of $38. In fact the extent to which the devaluation reversed the trend against the dollar was negligible. There was some covering of short positions, but soon after the turn of the year the dollar came once more under selling pressure. Apart altogether from the anticipation of a second devaluation, its earlier appreciation to the vicinity of its new maximum support points encouraged speculators to go short in anticipation of its depreciation by some $4\frac{1}{2}$ per cent, to its minimum support points, even in the absence of another devaluation.

CHAPTER FIFTEEN

The Case Against the Floating Dollar

THE restabilisation of the dollar after the suspension of its convertibility may be followed by a period of frequent minor changes of parities of important currencies. These changes may assume the form of statutory devaluations and revaluations periods of floating. Or there may be *de facto* changes of the support points at which various Governments will hold the actual exchange rates of their respective currencies, independently of their nominal gold parities. The present chapter aims at examining the situation that would be created by the adoption of floating exchanges in the real sense of the term.

There is no rigid borderline between the two systems. In almost every instance of floating exchanges the authorities intervened when they took the view that the exchanges floated too far, or that the direction, extent or tempo of their free floating was not in accordance with their wishes. The difference between such interventions and the setting up of relatively rigid if temporary new support points which are apt to be changed frequently in practice is merely one of degree, even though in theory they are supposed to constitute different systems.

Fanatically dogmatic believers in the theory that if exchanges are left alone they are bound to float to their trade equilibrium levels are strongly opposed to any official intervention to influence floating rates. Professor Schiller coined the phrase 'dirty floating' to express his condemnation of any attempt to interfere with market influences – conveniently forgetting that he himself and his predecessors intervened on a very large scale to influence the floating of the Deutschemark. But most advocates of the system of floating exchanges are prepared to concede the need for some degree of intervention in given circumstances.

Yet in trying to combine extreme flexibility with intervention they are admittedly guilty of gross inconsistency, even if 'dirty floating' is too strong a term to use in condemning it. Those advocates of floating exchanges who favour that system on the basis of their superstitious belief that if left to their own devices exchange rates would float to their equilibrium levels, are at any rate consistent in opposing intervention.

This highly involved and technical subject is examined in detail in my book entitled *The Case against Floating Exchanges*. It tries to prove that the advocacy of the system is based on an elementary logical fallacy, resting as it does on the false implied assumption that all foreign exchange transactions are derived from foreign trade. Even on that unrealistic and obviously incorrect assumption the theory is subject to several major reservations, the most important amongst them being the ever-changing time-lags between commerical transactions and their actual effect on the foreign exchange market in the form of increases or reductions in the volume of supply of, or demand for, foreign exchanges.

But assuming, for the sake of argument, that no such time lag exists, the impact of foreign trade on exchange rates is liable to be offset or stepped up by the influence of foreign exchange transactions of a non-commercial origin – discrepancies between supply and demand originating from capital movements, speculation, arbitrage and Governmental receipts or payments in foreign countries.

Even assuming for the sake of argument that there is an exchange rate at which American visible and invisible imports would be balanced by American visible and invisible exports, there would be quite a different equilibrium rate at which dollar transactions arising from short-term capital movements would balance, yet another rate at which speculative buyers and sellers would offset each other, and quite a different rate at which arbitrage would come to a standstill, or at which buying or selling through arbitrage would offset each other. There would be no conceivable equilibrium rate for the Government's foreign exchange or, for that matter, for private long-term capital transactions, even if there may be an equilibrium level for short-term movements of balances and credits.

Since it is utterly unlikely that the same rate would ever be the equilibrium level for all these different transactions, it stands to reason that the exchange rate tends to be diverted by non-commercial transaction all the time from the rate at which imports and exports would tend to be in theory at equilibrium. This means that in the absence of official intervention in the market by the American authorities or by foreign authorities, the floating dollar could not possibly be expected ever to float automatically to a level at which American imports and exports would tend to balance, except perhaps by sheer coincidence and quite temporarily. For if the dollar is at its trade equilibrium rate it would not equate transaction arising from capital movements, speculation, arbitrage, or Government receipts and payments abroad. Any of these transactions are liable to divert the rate from its trade equilibrium level.

Of course it is arguable that Government intervention should be confined to counteracting the effect of non-commercial influences which tend to divert the dollar from its trade equilibrium level. The trouble is that the authorities cannot reasonably be expected to be omniscient. They have no means of knowing even approximately the whereabouts of trade equilibrium rates. When we talk about overvalued and undervalued exchange rates we are far from being in the realm of exact science. Unless an exchange is grossly undervalued or over-valued our judgment might well be mistaken. It is only when the overvaluation or undervaluation is quite obvious – as in the early '70s in the case of the yen and of the dollar – that the authorities are safe in assuming that an exchange rate has deviated from its trade equilibrium level. For this reason, the if policy is adopted that intervention should be confined to counteracting deviations from trade equilibrium level the execution of that policy must necessarily be based on sheer guessing, unless exchanges are quite obviously influenced by some ascertainable cause.

From earlier remarks it appears that it was a mistake to

expect a floating dollar to adjust itself to its trade equilibrium level unless the process of adjustment was assisted by official intervention. In the case of the United States – as indeed in the case of all countries – the restoration of the balance of payments is not a simple adjustment of the rate to a level at which imports and exports would balance. Given the extent of Government spending abroad (especially military expenditure, which would remain high even after the withdrawal of American Forces from Vietnam, but also foreign aid) the United States must have a substantial surplus on current trading account, as indeed she had until recently, in order to maintain or restore equilibrium of her balance of payments. Unless capital import and export happen to offset each other, any surplus or deficiency arising from capital movements would also have to be offset by a corresponding deficiency or surplus on current trading account.

The dollar would have to float, or it would have to be adjusted – either through intervention by the American authorities or through changes of parities, or through invervention by foreign Governments – to a level at which there is an adequate surplus on current trading account to meet any deficiency on other accounts. Moreover, there is a difference between commercial equilibrium on paper – that is, in the trade returns – and in the foreign exchange market where payments affecting supply and demand hardly ever coincide with the arrival or departure of goods. Raw materials and consumer goods are usually paid in cash or are financed with the aid of three months' credits, while capital goods are financed with the aid of long-term loans. If as a result of a change in the exchange rate an increase of the imports of consumer goods is balanced by an increase in the exports of capital goods commercial demand for foreign exchanges would continue to exceed commercial supply, because of the difference in the terms of payment.

There is also the speculative factor to be considered. In his declaration of 15 August 1971 President Nixon stated and even overstated the influence of speculation on the dollar. Yet a month later Mr Connally, in his speech at the annual meeting of the IMF, insisted that exchanges must be allowed to float freely in order that they should reach a level at which the American deficit is eliminated. He seems to have overlooked that speculation is liable to cause exchange rates to deviate from their trade equilibrium level to a considerable extent and for prolonged periods. Such deviations are in turn liable to change the trade equilibrium level as a result of causing an overvaluation or an undervaluation of a floating dollar.

In an ideal world the authorities would be able to ascertain the extent to which an exchange movement is due to speculation – or, for that matter, to changes in leads and lags or in hedging – and they could intervene to offset the deviation from equilibrium level. In our world these factors cannot be isolated from movements due to changes in the volume and value of commercial transactions. The time lag between foreign trade transactions and their appearance in trade returns is one of the many reasons why it is impossible for the authorities to ascertain the extent to which exchange rates are influenced by noncommercial factors. Even if the efficient use of computers were to enable the authorities to follow the trade balance closely day after day it would not help adequately, for they would still be unable to ascertain when imports and exports produce their effects on supply and demand in the foreign exchange market.

Advocates of floating exchanges assume that under the system of their choice there would be much less speculation than under fixed parities. This belief is entirely mistaken. Admittedly, when a fixed currency is widely considered to be grossly overvalued or undervalued, and is therefore distinctly devaluation-prone or revaluation-prone, sweeping speculative movements are liable to arise. But the extent of such movements is liable to be mitigated by the belief held by a high proportion of those concerned that the Government is determined and able to maintain the exchange within support points. Under freely floating exchanges it is the Government's declared policy not to resist buying or selling pressure. Whenever such pressure develops – whether through speculation or other causes – a much higher proportion of those concerned assume therefore that the pressure would not be resisted. More speculators are tempted to take a hand if they have no cause to fear intervention.

Under the system of fixed exchanges the majority of importers and exporters do not cover their exchange risk unless there appears to be some obvious reason that makes it expedient to do so. Under the system of floating exchanges, on the other hand, it is considered advisable to make it a standing rule to cover whenever there appear to be indications of an exchange movement. This alone is liable to affect exchange rates through changes in leads and lags, changes which tend to be more extensive than under fixed exchanges.

Floating exchanges are liable to be subject to more self-aggravating trends than exchanges with fixed parities, precisely because of the widespread assumption, referred to above, that the authorities are less likely to intervene to offset them. Under fixed parities it is their duty to do so once the dollar has reached support points. Under the floating system it depends entirely on the policy and tactics the authorities choose to pursue. It is entirely unpredictable whether pressure on the exchange would be resisted or would be allowed to produce its effect. Indeed it is even conceivable that intervention might aim at reinforcing the movement in progress. This actually happened in 1969 when the Bundesbank intervened to reinforce the appreciation of the Deutschemark. On the assumption that the movement would not be resisted many more speculators, investors and traders would buy an appreciation-prone currency and sell a depreciation-prone currency. Under fixed parities once an exchange has reached its fixed support point, only those who do not believe in the Government's determination or ability to hold it there deem it necessary or advantageous to swim with the prevailing tide.

Under fixed parities there was close co-operation between the Federal Reserve and foreign Central Banks to co-ordinate their intervention as a matter of routine. There may of course be co-operation between monetary authorities also under floating exchanges, provided that they happen to agree on the extent to which their respective exchanges should be allowed to appreciate or depreciate. In the absence of such agreement the monetary authorities of various countries are liable to intervene at cross-purposes. They might operate against each other, as they often did during the '30s. Of course if as a result of lack of co-ordination two monetary authorities intervene at different rates they might give free gifts to arbitrageurs who are able to buy a currency from one authority and sell it to another authority at a higher rate. This would reduce intervention to absurdity. Central Banks may be unable to intervene even if they deem it necessary to do so, because they would clash with the intervention of other Central Banks.

It would take a volume to list all the disadvantages to which America would be exposed under a system of floating dollars. Some of these disadvantages would soon become obvious within a very short time, others may not be discovered until the advent of certain gravely disturbing circumstances. But I am convinced that as a result of the very brief experience with the floating exchanges there is now considerably less enthusiasm for floating exchanges than there was before the suspension of Bretton Woods stability.

CHAPTER SIXTEEN

The Monetary Power Vacuum

IN an old-world village a yokel was asked by a visitor to tell him who was the oldest inhabitant. 'He died last week and now we 'aint got one,' was the unexpected reply. Silly as this answer may sound, it happens to represent exactly the present position in the international monetary sphere. If anyone asked me which currency is best suited to serve as the reserve currency I would have to answer in terms similar to those used by the simple-minded villager: 'The dollar is no longer suitable and now we haven't got a currency which would be suitable to take its place.'

In other words, there is now what may be described as power vacuum in the international monetary sphere. The dollar ceased to qualify for the role of reserve currency long before it deliberately abdicated from that role on August 15, 1971. It continued to be used as a reserve currency for want of any better.

For years before Mr Nixon's epoch-making declaration of 15 August 1971 the dollar was used as the principal reserve currency long after it ceased to be really suitable for playing that role. From March 1968, when the two-tier gold price system came into being, until August 1971 it was a matter of common knowledge that, although in theory the dollar was supposed to be convertible into gold for foreign Governments and Central Banks, in practice the United States would refuse to comply with this obligation if some Central Bank should demand an embarrassingly large amount. Its conversion into gold for official holders ceased in 1968 to be a matter of routine. It became a matter of negotiation.

Moreover, from time to time, the dollar came to be considered devaluation-prone, either because of its own weakness or because of selling pressure on it due to the strength of some revaluation-prone currency. Admittedly, sterling, too, continued for years to play the part of reserve currency in spite of having been considered very devaluation-prone over prolonged periods. But that role came to be confined largely to the Sterling Area.

Yet another reason why the dollar ceased to be qualified to serve the role as a reserve currency early in 1971 was that Mr Nixon appeared to have given priority to electioneering considerations over the need for defending the dollar by resisting inflation. The moment he reversed his deflationary policy in spite of the escalation of wage inflation in the United States the dollar became obviously unsuitable for continuing to play the part of a reserve currency, in the same way as sterling came to be disqualified by the priority given by British Governments to pleasing the electorate over defending sterling. Admittedly, the adoption of a policy of income-restraint and price-restraint resorted to by Mr Nixon is liable to make up for the abandonment of the credit squeeze. But the success of the new experiment is unpredictable.

Finally the dollar became less and less suitable to fulfil that role, as a result of the spectacular increase of the amount of dollars held abroad. According to Chapter One of almost every elementary textbook on money, an object, in order to qualify for being used as money, must have scarcity value. During the early post-war years the dollar did meet that requirement more than sufficiently. There was a world-wide scarcity of dollars. It took the prophetic vision of Keynes to envisage, in his last article written shortly before his death and published in the *Economic Journal* of June 1946, the possibility that dollars might not continue to remain scarce till doomsday. By the middle of the '60s the dollar was no longer scarce and by the late '60s it became over-abundant.

In addition to the large holdings of dollars by Central Banks, private holdings by non-residents increased to near-astronomic figures through the development and expansion of the Euro-dollar market described in Chapter 6. On the face of it the existence of some $60 billion held by non-residents in the form of Euro-dollar deposits should not have disqualified the dollar from serving as a reserve currency held by Central Banks. But the mere existence of such large holdings which could be thrown on the foreign exchange market at any moment whenever the dollar's stability came to be doubted made the dollar very vulnerable. We saw in Chapter 6 that Euro-dollars provided considerable additional means for speculating against the dollar.

With the adoption of floating exchanges by the United States the dollar abandoned its claim to be qualified for the role of a reserve currency. It is true, since the reserves had to be held in some form and since not enough monetary gold was available for that purpose, it had to be held in the form of some currency. Since no stable currency or composite unit was available or was suitable for the purpose, Central Banks and private interests had to hold their reserves willy nilly in an unsuitable currency. The choice was between currencies which were considered to be the least likely to depreciate. But since it was the declared policy of the United States Government to depreciate the dollar in terms of other currencies it was less trustworthy than some other floating currencies belonging to a country the government of which did not aim at its depreciation and which was liable to appreciate.

Although the United States aimed at upholding the fiction of maintaining the dollar's gold parity nominally unchanged at the figure of $35 this make-believe did not alter the deplorable fact that the dollar was officially inconvertible into gold at any price, and that the officially declared American policy aimed at its depreciation in terms of other currencies, if not in terms of gold. Central Banks continued to hold their dollar reserve merely because they were reluctant to cut their losses by buying gold or some more trustworthy currency at free market prices and because there was in fact no alternative reserve currency. It is true, there were several strong currencies which were more confidence-inspiring than the dollar, but none of them was considered suitable for assuming the role hitherto played by the dollar. The position remained the same after realignment.

There is in the first instance the Deutschemark. It is by far the strongest currency at the time of writing, with the possible exception of the yen and the Swiss franc. It tended to rise in value, minor interruptions apart, after it became a floating currency in May 1971, and it was expected to continue to rise. But the West German Government is opposed to the Deutschemark becoming a reserve currency. It has adopted various measures to discourage its acquisition by foreign holders. This in spite of the temptation to take advantage of the strength of the Deutschemark for the increase of Germany's power and influence in world affairs.

In this connection we must draw attention to one of the major changes that occurred since the war – that countries have become more powerful and influential without possessing formidable military power. Before the war the standing of Great Powers was determined by their military strength. Today, even though neither Germany nor Japan can of course be compared with the military strength of super-Powers, – the United States or Soviet Russia – or even with that of communist China, they certainly play a leading part among powers of the second rank. In the Common Market Germany and France compete for the leading role on a more or less equal footing in spite of the fact that France is much better armed than Germany. This is because Germany's superior economic power makes up for the difference. If the Deutschemark should become a reserve currency and should come to play the part of the leading international currency in the place of the dollar the resulting increase of Germany's power might well tip the balance in her favour. Notwithstanding this the West German Government is opposed to adopting the policy of *Deutschemark Deutschemark Über Alles*, for fear that the German economy would then become too vulnerable to international influences.

Tempting as it may have appeared to the Government of Bonn to achieve German supremacy in the international monetary sphere, so far it has resisted the temptation. Considerations of prestige and political power have not prevailed over considerations of economic interests which have made it appear expedient to prevent or at any rate mitigate the landslide-like influx of foreign funds escaping from the dollar. The main reason for this attitude lies in the inflationary effect of such influx. Having had more than their fair share of advanced inflation in the past, the Germans prefer to err on the side of caution and to renounce financial power and glory for the sake of financial stability and security. Moreover the German authorities have enough common sense to realise that hot money is liable to go out as easily as it has come in, and that it might go out at the wrong moment.

Having regard to the fact that Germany is not keen on taking over the role of the United States in the international monetary sphere it is hardly surprising that Switzerland should be even less keen on assuming that role. She has no political ambitions whatsoever beyond retaining her neutrality, and it is doubtful whether a country of her size could play an important part in the political sphere even if it possessed the leading international currency. Moreover the dimensions of her domestic economy are infinitesimal compared with those of Germany, let alone those of the United States. For this reason international influences could easily play havoc with her domestic economy. Hence the persistent efforts made by Switzerland to keep down as far as possible the international use of the Swiss franc.

Although the yen is now very strong and the Japanese are a very proud nation, rightly proud of their economic recovery and expansion, the last thing the Japanese Government would want is that the yen should assume the role of the leading international reserve currency. It is possible that the reason, or at any rate one of the reasons, why the various measures of exchange restrictions and credit restrictions adopted by Japan originally to safeguard the yen against adverse pressure have been maintained after the turn of the tide, in spite of the perennial export surplus and the greatly increased reserves, is to discourage an unwanted influx of foreign funds. Since the developments that followed the change in the status of the dollar these restrictions have been further reinforced to a considerable extent.

While the German and Swiss restrictions are directed solely against an influx, Japanese restrictions operate both ways. Even though balances on foreign accounts may be withdrawn, this is a very effective way of discouraging any influx because a great many people would hesitate to transfer money to a country which might conceivably prevent them from withdrawing it. Another difference between Japan and other countries is that while practically every country welcomes the influx of long-term capital Japan maintains a ban even on foreign direct investments.

The reason why Germany and Japan adopted floating exchanges was to discourage the influx of foreign funds. The same consideration did not apply to Switzerland; she is even more afraid of instability of her currency under a floating system than of the influx of foreign money.

The French franc became another strong currency in the early '70s, even though its troubles as a result of the disturbances in May and June 1968 are still fresh in human memory. Before those disturbances France was harbouring the ambition to achieve for the French franc the role of leading international currency. For a number of years up to the middle of 1968 the franc was indeed a strong currency, partly as a result of the discipline enforced by de Gaulle, but largely because of whole-sale repatriations of French money from abroad after the settlement of the Algerian crisis and its aftermaths. At the beginning of 1968 almost all exchange control measures were removed, possibly in order to prepare Paris for assuming the role of the leading international financial centre. Simultaneously France was doing her best to weaken and discredit the dollar. For a short time the franc was the strongest currency, but the political and social upheaval in May and June 1968 reduced it for some time into the weakest major currency in a matter of a few weeks. It remained weak until its efficiently planned and executed devaluation in 1969.

This experience conclusively proves that the franc is not suitable to play the role of an international reserve currency. When de Gaulle and M. Pompidou vetoed Britain's entry into the

Common Market on the ground that sterling was too vulnerable because of its international role they appeared to have over-looked that the franc was even more vulnerable because of the utter lack of financial patriotism of the French people. Even though British exchange restrictions preventing UK residents from transferring their money abroad are not exactly water-tight, compared with them French exchange restrictions are simply non-existent. In Britain only an insignificant fraction of residents practise evasion of exchange control. In France all the upper classes and upper middle classes are doing it as a matter of course, and even menbers of the lower middle classes and upper working classes like to have some sort of hedge against a depreci-ation of the franc. Whenever the franc comes under a cloud there is a gigantic flight of domestic capital comparable in size with any flight of foreign capital from the financial centre of a country whose currency is a reserve currency.

Until the summer of 1971 even the most extreme optimist could not have envisaged conditions in which sterling would ever be able to recover even part of its former role as a reserve currency. Yet Sterling Area Central Banks increased their sterling reserves during 1970 and 1971 well above the amounts guaranteed in terms of dollars under the Basle Agreement of 1968. Following on the currency chaos initiated by Mr Nixon's announcement, there were indications of a flight into sterling. Throughout the late months of 1971 there was a heavy influx enabling the British authorities to repay a substantial part of their outstanding debt to the IMF in addition to increasing their reserves to well above £2,000 million.

But what matters is not the benefit that sterling could derive from the flight from the dollar but its prospects of maintaining its strength. Will Britain be able to continue to have a favourable balance of payments long enough to restore basic confidence in sterling? At the time of writing this appears problematic, owing to the probability of major labour troubles and the continuation of the wage inflation.

There is no other currency which could even be considered as a candidate for assuming the role which the dollar is no longer capable of performing adequately. The question is, is the dollar itself likely to recover its strength sufficiently to become once more suitable to continue its role as a reserve currency?

Evidently Mr Nixon and his advisers hoped that other currencies would be revalued or would appreciate sufficiently to eliminate the trade deficit due to the overvaluation of the dollar. But they entertained no ambitions for the dollar ever to resume once more its old role, for the experience of the late '60s and the early '70s made them realise the disadvantages of that role. In any case, the effect of the revaluation or appreciation of other currencies might be offset by inflation in the United States; the possibility of restoring the dollar's old role could not be expected to arise until after the Presidential election.

It has been widely suggested that a composite European currency might be able to become a successful rival to the dollar, especially after Britain joined the Common Market. Some minor degree of integration is not outside the realm of possibilities, but the creation of a European currency would only be possible following on the economic and even political integration. But a unified European currency is a Utopian dream, and even if I were wrong about this it would not materialise for many years to come. Meanwhile some minor degree of integration under the Werner plan might further damage the dollar's chances without creating an alternative reserve currency. Under the first phase of the Werner plan the band between support points of EEC currencies would be narrower than the band between them and the dollar. Situations would be liable to arise in which EEC countries would use each other's currencies as intervention currencies instead of using the dollar as virtually the sole intervention currency. This would reduce their genuine requirements for dollars and it would provide an additional reason for aiming at a reduction of their dollar reserves.

Another suggestion was that Special Drawing Rights should be used extensively for the settlement of international claims. Their use would of course have to be confined to official holders.

A plan put forward formally by the Chancellor of the Exchequer, Mr Barber, at the September 1971 meeting of the IMF follows those lines. In view of its importance I propose to deal with it in Chapters 19 and 20. Thereafter I shall try to examine the possibilities of restoring the dollar to its rightful place.

CHAPTER SEVENTEEN

Back to Economic Nationalism

THE way in which advocates of floating exchanges pursue their crusade by trying to make us believe that black is white and *vice versa* compels reluctant admiration. They actually profess to believe that the system of their choice is a preferable alternative to economic nationalism which, according to them, would arise as surely as night follows day as a result of the maintenance of fixed parities. This contention is in flagrant conflict with generally known facts of recent history. There may be some excuse for the younger generation to ignore the experience of floating exchanges in the '30s which were accompanied by an increase of economic nationalism in the form of protectionism and exchange control. But the older generation of economists, and students of all ages concerned with inter-war economic history, cannot plead ignorance.

In his review in *The Economic Journal* of a volume of essays on flexible exchange rates, edited by G. N. Halm, Sir Roy Harrod describes the absence of any reference to the British experience with a managed floating exchange as 'a curious omission'. He states that the British inter-war experience was 'far and away the most important experience of this type during the twentieth century'. Of course it is quite understandable that advocates of floating exchanges should try to ignore the British pre-war experience out of existence, since it does not suit their thesis. For it conclusively proves that floating rates are not incompatible with economic nationalism. Anyhow, the experience of 1946–70, during which period the extent of economic nationalism came to be greatly reduced, thanks to stability achieved under the Bretton Woods system, is conclusive.

The floating of sterling after 1931 was accompanied by the

abandonment of Britain's traditional policy of free trade. When the dollar went off the gold standard two years later, there followed a period of competitive currency depreciation race in pursuit of the 'beggar-my-neighbour' game. The idea was to export unemployment to other countries. If that is not extreme economic nationalism the term has no meaning.

It took an almost super-human effort after the war by a number of Governments to remove or mitigate the tariff walls and other protectionist measures, and to moderate the degree of exchange control. The success of their effort was largely due to the Bretton Woods principles and their gradual application. Under the obligations undertaken by Governments that joined the IMF the elaborate apparatus of exchange controls was dismantled to a very high degree, at any rate as far as they applied to funds owned by non-residents. The stability of exchanges and the Bretton Woods spirit was largely responsible for the success of the Kennedy Rounds of tariff reductions and for the achievements of GATT.

Liberalisation of trade and exchanges owes at least as much to the Bretton Woods spirit as to the letter of the rules elaborated at Bretton Woods and in subsequent agreements. It was the Bretton Woods spirit that made co-operation between Governments a matter of routine and created a willingness of giving mutual assistance. Thanks to that spirit, very little of the pre-war 'beggar-my-neighbour' attitude survived. Yet before the war it was considered a matter of course that every country should look exclusively after its own interests, regardless of the effects of its policies on other countries. And it was no sheer coincidence that Mr Nixon, when announcing the abandonment of Bretton Woods stability, also enunciated his 'America for herself' doctrine.

Admittedly, during the Bretton Woods era the defence of overvalued parities induced several Governments to apply temporary protectionist measures and some degree of exchange controls. But it would be absurd to imagine that only fixed rates have to be defended by such measures. We already saw in Chapter 15 that in given circumstances floating rates, too, have to be defended, if they float excessively in an unwanted direction. Intervention under the floating system constitutes a powerful weapon in the armoury of economic nationalism.

The adoption of the floating dollar was accompanied by the adoption of the 10 per cent surcharge by the United States in violation of the GATT principles, which owe their existence to American initiative. It reversed the results of the Kennedy Rounds, which had been achieved thanks to American initiative. The adoption of the floating yen was accompanied by a tightening of the existing Japanese exchange controls. The adoption of the floating pound necessitated similar additional control measures. The examples could be multiplied, but those quoted here should suffice to discredit the contention that by adopting floating exchanges a relapse into pre-war economic isolationism and nationalism could be avoided.

So long as exchanges were maintained stable under the Bretton Woods system there was no need for safeguarding the domestic markets against exchange dumping. It is true, the United States adopted the surcharge mainly in order to prevent Japan from dumping vast quantities of goods on the American markets by underselling domestic goods thanks to her undervalued exchange rate, which was still fixed at the time. But the overvaluation of the dollar indicated a state of fundamental disequilibrium so that the United States would have been entitled under the Bretton Woods rules to devalue it by 10 per cent without even consulting the IMF. There would have been no outcry even about a bigger devaluation of the dollar, no ill-feeling on the part of Japan and other countries which would have been affected unfavourably by such a devaluation to a higher extent than they came to be affected by the 10 per cent surcharge. For while the surcharge remedied the overvaluation of the dollar in the American market only, a devaluation of the dollar would have remedied it in all markets.

In spite of this, Japan and other countries would have preferred a devaluation of the dollar to the imposition of a surcharge. It is true, in theory, exchange dumping could have ocurred also as a result of devaluations under the Bretton

Woods system. But what matters is that in actual practice it did not occur during the quarter century of its operation. At any rate no member Government complained. None of the devaluations carried out between 1947 and 1971 were followed by any retaliatory action leading to trade war or competitive devaluation race. Quite on the contrary, the Governments showed a high degree of understanding towards the circumstances of each other's devaluations. So far from opposing or resenting devaluations, on several occasions they urged the country in difficulty to solve its problem by devaluing. All this was in accordance with the Bretton Woods spirit.

Admittedly, member Governments also urged some Government from time to time to revalue in order to mitigate its own difficulties without having to devalue or deflate to that end. But the fact that on several occasions Germany and other countries were prepared deliberately to handicap themselves by revaluing their currencies indicates a high degree of realisation of the interdependence of nations, realisation that was conspicuous by its absence during the period of floating exchanges between the wars and again in August–December 1971.

The United States adopted the surcharge as a bargaining weapon to force other countries to revalue their currencies in accordance with her interests. But more than one country can play that game. It is true, the large import surplus of the United States on her trade with Japan placed her in a strong bargaining position, for American protectionist measures could damage Japanese trade much more than Japanese protectionist measures could damage American trade. Since, however, the United States had a surplus on her trade with the Common Market, retaliations from that direction were apt to hurt her.

Moreover, retaliations could assume other forms. Since the United States violated the GATT rules by imposing the surcharge (she is not the only leading country that violated them) other countries could have acted likewise by subsidising exports or by some other device which would hurt American exports. Even the surcharge itself and the appreciation of the floating yen in relation to the dollar might have recoiled on American trade. For Japan's exportable surpluses which came to be excluded from the United States were liable to be subsidised and dumped on other countries to the detriment of American export trade. While the competitive capacity of Japanese exports to the United States tended to be reduced as a result of the surcharge, it might have been maintained and even increased for exports to other countries. Frozen stocks were liable to be dumped on those markets at below cost, with or without Government subsidies.

Mr Nixon's measures of 15 August marked the beginning of a new era of economic nationalism and isolationism in the free world. Had the period of floating exchanges proved to be more than a purely temporary transition to be followed soon by a realignment of currencies, we would have an all-round tightening of exchange controls. A clear indication of this was provided by the legislation introduced in Switzerland to make certain restrictions hitherto based on a 'gentlemen's agreement' statutory. Considering that Switzerland had been for many years one of the very few countries which removed all restrictions on the outflow of capital, domestic or foreign, the adoption of such legislation constituted a symptom indicating the reversal of the world trend towards liberalisation. It was all the more significant as Switzerland attached immense importance to her role as a haven for refugee funds and her functions as one of the world's most important international banking centres.

The relapse into economic nationalism by the United States produced a demoralising effect all over the free world. There was a danger that co-operation in accordance with the Bretton Woods spirit might be replaced by the pre-war attitude of 'everybody for himself', to the detriment of all in the long run and even in the short run. In addition to an all-round tightening of exchange controls and an increase of tariff barriers by 'temporary' surcharges, there might have been a revival of a trend towards bilateral trading, in order to mitigate the difficulties created by exchange controls and protection. Quotas would reappear in due course. Fear of losing reserves through the overvaluation of their currencies or through measures of other

countries, dictated by economic nationalism, might have revived the exchange clearing system. There is much to be said
for it if applied to trading with countries behind the Iron
Curtain, but it would be a matter for regret if it came to be
applied in trading between countries of the free world.

During August–December, 1971, increased flexibility of exchanges manifested itself, in the case of most currencies other
than the dollar – one or two took the opportunity for devaluing
– in upward floating or revaluation. But adoption of safeguards
against an outflow of foreign hot money was well on the cards.
To safeguard against the effects of a reversal of the trend,
countries which were receiving hot money on a large scale in
anticipation of an appreciation of their currencies might have
felt the need to make advance provisions for defensive measures
when the trend turns.

Any currency which is revaluation-prone is apt to become
devaluation-prone at any moment, either through adverse developments within that country or through improvements in
other countries. The size of recent influx of hot moneys into
some countries in anticipation of revaluations or upward floating is quite without precedent. The presence of a large volume of hot money is always a source of potential weakness,
even though its influx reinforces temporarily the reserves. This
explains why the increase of Britain's reserves in 1971 failed to
inspire an unqualified confidence in sterling in the long run.
After all, the amounts borrowed by Britain from the IMF and
from foreign Central Banks were due to be repaid on certain
fixed dates, while the amounts that came to be owed to tens of
thousands of private holders of sterling assets are liable to be
withdrawn or sold forward at any moment.

Moreover, in possession of reserves in excess of immediate
requirements the receiving countries are tempted to use up a
high proportion of their surplus, either through over-exporting
capital by acquiring illiquid foreign investments, or through
relaxing restraint on the domestic economy, As a result, when
holders of hot money withdraw their balances the surplus
reserves created during the period of influx may no longer be

available. Few countries are in a strong enough position to disregard altogether the possibility of a turn of the tide of hot money.

Even a wholesale repatriation of residents' capital that had sought refuge abroad is a source of potential weakness, because of the ever-present possibility of another flight of domestic capital. We saw this happen in France in 1968. Had it not been for the repatriation of French capital in earlier years, there would not have been so much money available in 1968 to be sent abroad once more. While early in 1968 the French Government was seriously considering the idea of making Paris the leading financial centre, the strength of the franc evaporated in a matter of days in May 1968 as a result of the disturbances in France which reversed the influx of French capital. That kind of experience is liable to recur any time and anywhere, albeit to a varying degree. When a country revalues its currency or allows it to float upward as a result of the influx of funds, whether national or foreign, it increases the scope for its subsequent devaluation or depreciation as a result of a turn of the tide.

For this reason it may be deemed to be expedient to reinforce exchange control or trade restrictions when floating rates are adopted, or at any rate to make preparations enabling Governments to adopt the necessary measures at short notice. Such preparations foreshadow economic isolation. Governments seek powers to retaliate, if necessary, in a trade war or in case of disequilibrium through an overvaluation of their exchanges. And once they have those powers, it is often tempting to make use of them on the flimsiest excuse instead of aiming at strengthening the currency by pursuing sound policies.

Under floating exchanges there is strong inducement for reverting to exchange control affecting not only short-term balances but also long-term investment. It is liable to lead to a return of the system of multiple currencies under which certain types of foreign holders could only liquidate the proceeds of their holdings at a discount. France has already taken the first step by adopting the two-tier system. The uncertainty of the future prospects of most currencies and the possibility of exchange control is liable to discourage the Euro-issue market for medium- and long-term securities. Yet the emergence and expansion of that market during the '60s was one of the most promising developments from the point of view of international economic growth and of a better redistribution of capital resources.

The Euro-dollar market and other Euro-currency markets too are liable to suffer a reverse as a result of tighter controls or even the threat of tighter controls, also under the threat of changes in the exchange rates. It is true their expansion in recent years has been rather excessive. But the consolidation of that expansion is one thing, and its drastic reversal is quite another.

The falsity of the contention that floating exchanges tend to moderate economic nationalism is illustrated not only by the relapse into economic nationalism during the brief period of floating during August to December 1971 but also by the fact that, as a result of the return to fixed parities, the tide towards economic nationalism became immediately reversed. The United States repealed her protectionist measures simultaneously with the devaluation, and both Britain and Japan immediately mitigated the exchange restrictions which they reinforced after the initiation of the period of floating exchanges. Governments of other countries, too, came to the conclusion that under a system of fixed parities there was less need for exchange restrictions and trade restrictions than under a system of floating exchanges.

CHAPTER EIGHTEEN

Currency War or Compromise?

WE saw in the last chapter that in 1971 flexible exchanges revived economic nationalism. With his bombshell of 15 August 1971 President Nixon declared currency war and trade war to the rest of the free world. Instead of correcting the overvaluation of the dollar in the usual way, by devaluing it, he forced Governments all over the world to revalue their currencies or allow them to float upward, very much against their will. The alternative was to accumulate even more depreciation-prone dollars which he made completely inconvertible into gold. He refused to meet them halfway by devaluing the dollar at least to some extent. At the same time he imposed protectionist measures in defiance of undertakings given by ratifying GATT and in various other treaties. There was a real danger that this act of financial and commercial aggression might lead to a currency war and a trade war.

Fortunately it takes two parties to make war. In spite of the protests and accusations hurled at Mr Nixon from all sides, there were no retaliations. Such actions as were taken by various Governments were of a defensive nature. With few exceptions, they either complied with Mr Nixon's demand to some extent and allowed their exchanges to float upward in terms of dollars, or they revalued their currencies. Some measures were adopted in most countries to resist the influx of foreign balances, in order to keep down as far as possible the amounts of dollars their Central Banks had to acquire in their efforts to mitigate the appreciation of their currencies in terms of dollars.

It was the height of irresponsibility on the part of Mr Nixon to risk splitting the free world by provoking a currency war and a trade war instead of devaluing the dollar. Fortunately the

statesmen of other countries were more statesmanlike. Although
there was much talk about retaliatory action – mainly for
domestic consumption and in order to strengthen their bargaining position in the forthcoming negotiations – the European
Governments duly realised that much more was at stake than
mere loss of trade and mere currency complications. They were
aware of the growing difficulties of the United States caused
largely by her chronic balance of payments deficit and they
realised that she had to do something drastic to restore equilibrium. It was bound to hurt the countries which had benefited by the expansion of their American markets. They are
bound to lose much trade irrespective of the way in which the
American import surplus is reduced.

As far as EEC countries were concerned they had no moral
basis whatsoever for complaining, considering that their discrimination against imports from outside the Common Market
was necessarily damaging to important American interests. As
for Britain, having regard to the generous financial assistance
she received from the United States for many years, it would
have been gross ingratitude to turn against the United
States when she made a long-overdue effort to work out her
own salvation after saving many other countries, including
Britain.

In any case, the United States continued to hold most of
the trumps because of her disproportionate contribution to the
defence of the free world in general and to the defence of
Western Europe in particular.

There was a very real danger that a further deterioration
of the American financial situation might have forced the
United States to reduce her contribution below safety limits.
Moreover, any retaliation on the part of Europe might have
antagonised American public opinion to such extent that the
Government might have been impelled by political pressure to
reduce American forces stationed in Germany and in the
Mediterranean, if not withdraw them altogether. At the time of
writing that danger still exists but, in the absense of retaliations
leading to a deterioration of relations between Western Europe

and the United States, there seems to be some hope that reductions of American forces for reasons of budgetary economy as well as for balance of payments considerations might not be excessive.

One of the reasons why the European Governments abstained from retaliation was the hope that a drastic improvement of the American balance of payments situation might lead to an early relaxation of the protectionist measures adopted by Mr Nixon, and that some form of compromise might be arrived at both in the monetary sphere and in the commercial sphere. It was realised that currency war and trade war would be wars in which both sides would lose.

Having regard to the fact that the European Governments were in any case not in a very good position to retaliate, it was a pity that so much unnecessary and futile heat was generated in their reactions to Mr Nixon's measures. This ill-advised attitude was greatly encouraged by many economists who had invented pseudo-theoretical justification for the obviously absurd demand by politicians that the United States should continue to have a gigantic balance of payments deficit for the sake of providing other countries with the required amount of international liquidity.

Economists subscribing to this theory must be held responsible for the brazen impudence with which the nine non-American Governments represented at the London meeting of Finance Ministers of the Group of Ten after Mr Nixon's statement demanded it as their rights that the United States should continue to remain in deficit, even though they graciously consented to its gradual reduction. Mr Connally treated this attitude with the contempt it deserved. For, apart altogether from the risk of a split in the free world which such a demand entailed, it was unwarranted also from a purely economic point of view. It was based on the logical fallacy of putting the cart before the horse. The main purpose of holding liquid international reserves is to meet balance of payments deficits. It was obvious that an increase of the American balance of payments deficit increased the world's total reserve *requirements* so that the creation of additional liquid reserves was merely sufficient to meet the additional requirements. While it resulted in a redistribution of international reserves, considering that they were transferred from a deficit country which needed them the most to surplus countries which needed them the least, the result was distinctly a maldistribution. We heard this term many times between the wars when European economists blamed the maldistribution of gold as one of the main causes of the world's economic difficulties. At that time the maldistribution assumed the form of the accumulation of formerly European international gold reserves by the United States. Now that it has assumed the form of increasing European international liquid reserves at the expense of the United States the argument which was valid in the '20s and the '30s is just as valid.

Politicians and economists seem to have forgotten that the globe was a reasonably happy planet during the long years when the United States had a large surplus on her current account and the British balance of payments had its ups and downs without any definite trend. Yet there was no stagnation for lack of international liquidity. Foreign trade continued to expand and, judging by that and by the rise in world prices, there must have been a surplus of liquidity rather than a deficiency. It is of course arguable that in the meantime the volume of foreign trade has increased very considerably, so that much more international liquidity is now required than fifteen years ago. But those who argue on such lines must be reminded that in the meantime Euro-dollars to the amount of some $60 billion have been created, in addition to other Euro-currencies, increases of IMF drawing rights, reciprocal swap arrangements, allocation of SDRs and even some increase in the world's monetary stocks of gold.

In any case, if international trade could only expand at the cost of a further deterioration of the financial power of the United States, it would be preferable to call a halt to the expansion. The world seems to be hypnotised by the fanatical belief in the need for a growing volume of foreign trade, expanding at an ever-accelerating pace. A little consolidation after a quarter century of spectacular expansion would do more good than harm.

Even if this should mean stagnation in the volume of domestic production – which need not be necessarily the case – there is much to be said for a little consolidation in that sphere, too. To those suffering from growth-hysteria this might sound worse than blasphemy. Yet there are indications of an increasing realisation that there is another side of the picture – pollution, which is causing irreparable harm to the human race, and is liable to endanger its very survival. It would be worth while to call a halt to growth and elaborate effective means for resisting pollution before resuming growth. If the American measures should lead to a spell of stagnation providing a chance for anti-pollution measures then the right thing would happen for the wrong reason.

The demand that the United States should slow down her efforts to eliminate her balance of payments deficit is fully as ridiculous as the American demand that Japan must admit American capital and enterprise in spite of the fact that the current balance of payments is very strongly in favour of Japan. It is understandable if business concerns supporting sectional interests apply such arguments. But it is absolutely unpardonable for economists to provide such ammunition to politicians who themselves ought to know better and are only misled by economists because the latter give them exactly the advice they want to receive.

There was indeed very little that the Governments concerned could have done to retaliate to the suspension of the convertibility of the dollar. The application of Article IV of the IMF Rules concerning uniform changes in par values to enforce a devaluation of the dollar was mentioned as one of several possible devices. But such a move by the IMF could have been vetoed by the United States because it would require support by votes representing 80 per cent of voting power. An alternative action would have been the adoption of really water-tight exchange control. But this would have actually helped the United States to balance her trade. Since Japanese exporters were unable to sell their dollars they abstained from entering into new contracts for exporting to the United States, which was precisely what the United States wanted.

Perhaps the only effective counter-attack would have been the purchase of gold against dollars in the free market by Central Banks. It must have been particularly tempting for Japan for instance to resort to that action. For even though it would have inflicted a heavy loss on herself if she had to pay for the gold prices well in excess of $35 – and her pressing demand might have easily pushed up the market price of gold to $70 or above – the amount of losses would have been bearable if compared with the amount Japan has saved on defence expenditure since 1945. The advantage would have been the acquisition of a substantial gold reserve to take the place of her holding of inconvertible dollars. The resulting sharp rise in the market price of gold, provided that the price settled down at a high level, might have forced the United States Government to devalue the dollar adequately.

There is little doubt that some such action might have been taken by Japan or by some other large holder of dollars if the IMF meeting in September 1971 had ended in a deadlock. It would have created much ill-feeling. That this was avoided must have been largely due to the common ground created by the British plan of expanding the scope of SDRs submitted to the meeting by the Chancellor of the Exchequer, Mr Barber. Even though neither the United States nor other countries committed themselves to supporting it, it was widely regarded as a suitable basis for negotiation to arrive at some acceptable formula that would break the deadlock.

Pending the outcome of the ensuing discussions to work out the basic principles and all-important details of the proposed system, or of an alternative solution on somewhat similar lines, the Governments felt it to be their duty as well as in their interest to abstain from any action which would cause a further deterioration of the international atmosphere. The meeting ended in an atmosphere which created at any rate the possibility of reaching some compromise.

It was the absence of retaliation that opened the way for sensible discussions aimed at reaching some compromise. The atmosphere at the Washington meeting of the IMF at the end of September 1971 was distinctly more conciliatory than at the London meeting a fortnight earlier. Even Mr Connally did not throw his weight about to anything like the same extent as he did in London. But he remained adamant about the gold parity of $35 and came out definitely in favour of a demonetisation of gold and of freely floating exchanges pending their restabilisation at a level to which they happen to float under the conflicting influences of a variety of factors, including speculation. Those were not his words, but that is what his pronouncement on the subject amounted to. Even so, the door was left ajar, if not open, for some form of negotiated compromise.

Such a compromise was actually reached on 18 December 1971, at the Washington meeting of the Finance Ministers of the Group of Ten. It was an agreement which enabled each principal participant to claim success.

The United States managed to keep down to a minimum the devaluation of the dollar and succeeded in inducing her principal rivals to handicap themselves by revaluing their currencies. Promises of trade concessions were made, and there was good reason for expecting the adoption of a basic currency reform which would mean the allocation of very substantial amounts of SDRs to the United States and the consolidation of her short-term dollar liabilities.

Britain was compensated for the revaluation of sterling against the dollar by its devaluation against the yen and the Deutschemark and by the prospects of a consolidation of Sterling Area sterling balances. France succeeded in defeating the campaign in flavour of floating exchanges, while Germany succeeded in achieving the broadening of the 'band' from the 2 per cent fixed at Bretton Woods to $4\frac{1}{2}$ per cent. Over and above all, the danger of a trade war and of a currency war came to be removed.

CHAPTER NINETEEN

The British Plan

THERE can be little doubt that the presentation of the British formula for the creation of international liquidity on a truly large scale constituted the turning point in the crisis initiated by Mr Nixon's measures. In his statement on 15 August 1971 Mr Nixon himself hinted at the need for a fundamental revision of the international monetary system, but he did not indicate the nature of the reform he had in mind. There had been much vague talk about reforms involving an expansion of the scope of SDRs long before the IMF meeting. But it was left to Mr Barber to indicate the broad outlines of a concrete and, on the face of it, feasible proposal which might meet American requirements and which might conceivably be found acceptable also by the other leading nations.

Mr Barber's plan contained some points – such as widening of the margins between which exchanges would be permitted to fluctuate after the establishment of their adjusted parities – which have been widely canvassed for years. There have also been suggestions in many academic quarters and, more recently, among practical specialists, that SDRs should be developed into a form of international currency. The originality of the official British contribution towards the solution of the deadlock consisted of the actual formula, the outlines of which were proposed by Mr Barber in his statement in Washington on 28 September 1971.

Although there has been frequent reference to SDRs in practically every chapter of this book, in view of the importance the device has now assumed as a proposed solution on which there appears to be a large measure of agreement, it is necessary to deal with the system in greater detail. Mr Barber's proposal is based on the existing system of SDRs in a modified form. Our first step is, therefore, to summarise the existing system.

After prolonged and highly controversial negotiations an agreement was reached by the Board of Governors of the IMF at their annual meeting in September 1967 at Rio de Janeiro to supplement the drawing rights allotted to member countries of the IMF, through the creation of Special Drawing Rights, the use of which would be subject to much less strict rules than the use of the original facilities provided by the IMF. Whether amidst escalating world inflation this was a wise move or not may be a matter of opinion. Here we shall confine ourselves to a description of the mechanism, and since Mr Barber in his statement foreshadowed drastic modifications in its rules it would be pointless to go into all its sophisticated intricacies. It should be sufficient for our present purposes to confine ourselves largely to a description of the basic principles of the system that is now in existence.

The initial amount of SDRs was fixed at $9·5 billion, to be issued in three instalments, over a period of five years. $3.5 billion was issued in 1970, $3 billion in 1971 and the rest in 1972. All SDRs were to be issued to all participants in the IMF – unless they contracted out – in strict proportion to their quotas. No time limit is fixed for their repayment, and indeed there is no direct obligation of repayment, but the average of the SDRs participants are entitled to use must not exceed 70 per cent over a period of five years. This provision means that 70 per cent of the allocations to each participant may be treated as a free gift, even though the allocations are supposed to operate like a form of revolving credit which are to be drawn upon again and again.

The allocations are granted unconditionally. Participants use their SDRs by transferring them, through the intermediary of the IMF, to other participants in return for receiving an equivalent amount in currencies 'convertible in fact' – which means currencies actually convertible not into gold but into other currencies – or in their own currencies. Participants have to apply to the IMF and it is the IMF that decides which other participant is to convert their SDRs. The IMF is not entitled to refuse such applications or to question the applicant about the purpose for which he needs the currencies received against their SDRs, even though it is laid down that the SDRs should be used for meeting balance of payments deficits.

Although in a large measure the allocations of SDRs amount to free gifts, they do contain a credit element, for participants have to reconstitute at least part of the amount used, in order to keep within the average maximum of 70 per cent. This is the provision to which Mr Barber referred when stating: 'Some changes would be needed in the nature of the Special Drawing Rights and the rules governing their use. I am thinking in particular of the credit element at present contained in the Special Drawing Rights, and therefore of the reconstitution provision.' If he meant by this remark that reconstitution should be done away with altogether and there should be no limit whatsoever for the use of allocations, they would assume completely the nature of free gifts, given unconditionally and not subject to repayment.

Practically all participants include their holdings of SDRs – whether allotted to them originally or obtained subsequently through transfers by other participants – in their gold and foreign exchange reserves. The value of SDR units is fixed in terms of gold and is equal to one gold dollar, i.e. 0·888671 grams of fine gold. SDRs are not a liability of the IMF, even though the holdings are registered in the IMF's Special Drawing Accounts and the IMF itself holds substantial amounts. They are re-registered by the IMF from one participant's account to another participant's account. Their qualification for inclusion in monetary reserves of Central Banks lies solely in the assumption that they are converted unconditionally into convertible currencies by other participants if instructed by the IMF to do so. Participants are under obligation to convert other participants' SDRs up to twice the amount of their own allocations.

Participants are entitled to withdraw from participation at a moment's notice. If they hold SDRs in addition to their allocations after the deduction of any of their own SDRs they had exchanged against currencies the IMF ensures their immediate repayment and allocates the SDRs thus received to other members. If the withdrawing participants have a net liability they have to repay it within three years in half-yealy instalments.

In his statement Mr Barber said that the SDR scheme has made a good start and that 'there is much to be said for building on what we already have'. What he had in mind, however, is a modified SDR. And since he considered it pointless to have two kinds of SDRs. the proposed changes would also have to apply to existing SDRs.

The three main objective of the plan are the following:

(1) The SDR could become the monetary unit (Mr Barber and others use the rather affected term *numéraire*) in terms of which parities should be expressed and in relation to which currencies could be revalued or devalued.

(2) The SDR could become the main asset in which countries hold their reserves. As already observed, most countries – apart from those which have used up their allocations – hold part of their reserves in SDRs, in addition to gold and foreign currencies. In most cases currencies are still the major element. According to Mr Barber, eventually SDRs could become the major element, 'with currency holdings largely confined to working balances'. Writing before the announcement of the British plan, Signor Ossola suggested that it would take between ten and fifteen years for SDRs to become the main assets in monetary reserves.

(3) Mr Barber advocates the controlled creation of adequate but not excessive world liquidity 'so as to become independent for the volume of liquidity on the deficit position of one or more countries'. He said that this was the intention of the existing SDR scheme, so that the new proposals would merely step up its application.

'A system on these lines would provide for, and indeed promote, appropriate adjustment by all countries – those in surplus as well as those in deficit – in order to maintain equilibrium, and so avoid one of the unsatisfactory features of the present system.'

Some of the main features of the existing SDR system would

be retained. Thus, it would still be held and exchanged only by Central Banks and monetary authorities. National currencies would remain the medium for ordinary trading in the foreign exchange markets and in the private sectors in general, also for official intervention in the foreign exchange markets. But Mr Barber suggests that for these purposes wider use might develop of currencies other than the dollar. He admits that 'Central Banks would continue to need working balances of currencies'. But he expects that in the course of time these requirements should be reduced 'to a reasonable working level'.

Mr Barber thinks that the reform would improve the scope for international control over the creation of new international liquidity and that it would help to remove some unspecified faults of the existing system, while reviving 'some of the best elements in the Bretton Woods concept'. This passage, like several other passages, is rather vague and does not indicate what the British plan has in mind.

All these points are concerned with a projected long-run reform. The following passage, however, has direct bearing on the immediate situation:

'In regard to parities, the unique problem for one currency, the US dollar, would disappear. The parity of the dollar would be expressed in terms of SDR in the same way as any other currency. This would give the United States Government an important instrument of adjustment policy which it has hitherto ruled out, that is, the possibility of changing the parity of its currency in the same way as other countries, subject to the same machinery of international agreement through the IMF. I would think that this freedom would be welcome to the United States.'

What he presumably means is that, once the dollar's parity is fixed in terms of SDRs, like that of all other currencies, the United States would no longer feel inhibited from changing her parity. The intention was evidently to provide a face-saving formula that would enable the United States to devalue the dollar as part of a major parity readjustment. This would indeed be an ideal way out of the deadlock.

The snag was that it could well take years before the new

plan was worked out and accepted – it took five years from the conception of the original SDR scheme till its final adoption – and the readjustment of parities was very urgent. The currencies could not be allowed to float while the experts of the leading countries worked out the innumerable details and while the politicians haggled over the terms of an agreement on the formula and its detailed application recommended by the experts. Fortunately the difficulty was overcome by the agreement of December 1971 providing for the immediate stabilisation of the main currencies at agreed new parities, with a widened spread. Had Mr Nixon insisted on a simultaneous conclusion of an agreement on the lines of Mr Barber's proposals, the free world would have been condemned to prolonged currency instability with all the disadvantages and risks it involved. Admittedly, during the four months of floating period between 15 August and 20 December there was no major disaster. But this was because there were no major political or economic crises which would have been aggravated by violent exchange movements. It was possible for the Governments concerned to keep the floating of rates within relatively narrow limits. There happened to be no political crises, no war scares, no violent social disturbances, no wholesale bankruptcies to cause panic in the foreign exchange markets.

Nevertheless, it is easy to imagine what would have happened if the dollar had been a floating currency during the crisis over Cuba, or if the French franc had been a floating currency during the crisis over Algeria or during the troubles of 1968. Nothing would have prevented a sweeping flight from the dollar or from the franc into currencies which would have been free to appreciate. The wild fluctuations of the '20s and the '30s would have repeated themselves.

In the absence of acute political or economic crises the world was spared the worst effects of exchange instability. Advocates of floating exchanges had no cause, however, for congratulating themselves. For even though fluctuations were kept under control, banks were beginning to find it difficult to provide the forward exchange facilities to their customers. This was partly because of official ceilings on their forward commitments and partly because of self-imposed limitations on their commitments in particular currencies or in particular countries, owing to the possibility of additional exchange control measures.

The world economy was beginning to experience a creeping paralysis, largely because of the discouraging effect of uncertainty on investment. Industrial firms were becoming increasingly reluctant to spend on the expansion or modernisation of their plant, owing to the uncertainty of exchange rates and owing to the possibility of a trade war. Had the difficulty of arriving at an agreement on the SDR system delayed the restabilisation a world depression might have developed. The increasing figures of shipping tonnage laid up, which are the most sensitive barometer, gave cause to concern.

Moreover, there was an ever-present possibility of some major political crisis or social disturbance. The absence of any such trouble during four months did not justify complacency. It was indeed fortunate that the Governments concerned agreed in December 1971 to deal with the immediate situation and defer the discussions on SDRs. Thanks to this decision, the British plan, instead of being an obstacle to a speedy settlement of the immediate problem, greatly contributed towards it. One of the main reasons why the United States Government adopted a more conciliatory attitude was its hope to obtain substantial SDR allocations in due course.

Nothing I have said above in favour of the British plan should be interpreted as indicating a change in my conviction that what we need is a major devaluation of the dollar and an adjustment of the parities of other currencies to the new dollar parity. Since, however, quite evidently that is out of the question unless and until some disastrous crisis would force the United States eventually to adopt that solution, the palliative adopted in December 1971 was a great improvement on the situation that existed after Mr Nixon's declaration, indeed since the Deutschemark became a floating exchange.

CHAPTER TWENTY

Pitfalls of the SDR Scheme

IN an ideal world the formula proposed by Mr Barber would undoubtedly provide a perfect solution of regulating world liquidity. We could trust the Ten Wise Men to determine the amount of SDRs in a way as to ensure stability combined with progress. In our imperfect world, however, the plan is open to objections. As France is the only leading country which is still trying to aim at upholding financial sanity, I sincerely hope that her spokesmen will do their utmost in the course of the negotiations about the plan and in the course of its application to ensure the adoption of adequate safeguards against the misuse of the new facilities.

It is impossible to criticise the British Plan adequately until we know much more about its details. As already remarked in the last chapter, several points in Mr Barber's statement are very vague even on its principles. Possibly he kept his statement deliberately vague and non-committal so as to avoid being too controversial at that stage. In his Introduction to his book *Remaking the International Monetary System* Professor Machlup confesses to having felt tempted to give his book the sub-title *Or, How to Get Agreement by Avoiding Excessively Clear Language*. If Mr Barber had gone into details he would almost certainly have provoked disagreement on the part of several speakers who followed him. As it was they could afford to indicate vaguely their broad agreement on the basic suggestion that some such reform would indeed be helpful. In any case, even if Mr Barber had gone into great details, the plan would undergo many changes in the course of its discussion by the Governments and Central Banks concerned.

To appreciate the significance of the reform and to be able to discover any possible pitfalls in it we would have to know a great deal more than what was said on 28 September. For instance we should like to know what 'changes' Mr Barber advocates in the credit element and in the reconstitution provisions of the existing SDRs system. Does he mean that the credit element is to be removed altogether or merely reduced? Does he mean that the need for ever reconstituting the original allocations by Central Banks which made use of them for converting their SDRs into currencies would cease, or merely that the terms of the reconstitution provisions would be made even softer? If the credit element is removed altogether, so that participants would not have ever to reconstitute their allocations, it would mean that allocations would become entirely free gifts. Even under the present system 70 per cent of the allocations may be considered as such. Would the proportion be raised to 100 per cent under the new rules?

This would raise once more the controversy which had to be fought out before the Rio agreement in 1967 – whether allocations should be made dependent on balance of payments requirements, or some other form of 'means test', or whether they should continue to be made in proportion of the quotas of participants. Since the richest nations have the largest quotas this would give cause for complaints by undeveloped countries. Even as it is, the present SDR scheme is based very much on the principle that 'he who hath shall be given'. If the credit element were removed altogether, or even reduced, it would further reinforce the complaint that the rich nations allocate free gifts to themselves, all the more since the amounts of SDRs are expected to increase very considerably.

There is however another side to this question. The United States and Britain have the largest quotas – 21·80 per cent and 10·36 per cent respectively – so that the allocation of large amounts of SDRs would enable them to reduce the amounts of dollars and sterling held in the reserves of Central Banks. Until the excessive dollar and sterling reserves were reduced to normal proportion there would be a case for the unequal distribution of the newly issued SDRs – unless some other acceptable formula is found for speeding up their reduction.

Mr Barber predicted that in the course of time SDRs would constitute the major part of Central Banks' reserves. Presumably he has a much shorter period in mind than the ten to fifteen years envisaged by Signor Ossola.

The prospects of a very large increase in the total of SDRs have created an entirely new situation. The fact that the existing system has worked satisfactorily on a small scale does not prove by itself that no new major problems would arise if the amount involved were to run into tens of billions of units. The $9\frac{1}{2}$ billion units allotted up to the time of writing were a mere drop in the ocean. Should the amount increase, say, tenfold it might aggravate the international inflationary trend and it would be certain to weaken further what has remained of the old balance of payments discipline. The fact that the first allocation was made when the escalation of the world-wide rise in wages and prices was gathering momentum does not augur very well for the enlarged edition of the scheme, at any rate from this point of view.

Increases of allocation would depend on a Board of Governors consisting of politicians who between them must represent at least 85 per cent of the total voting rights. Beyond doubt even this might be an improvement on a system in which international liquidity depends on the balance of payments deficits of countries with reserve currencies. That is to say, it *would be* an improvement if such a system really existed anywhere else than in the fertile imagination of some economists, Central Bankers and politicians. But as already observed in Chapter 18 the world was doing reasonably well before giant dollar deficits – or, for that matter, sterling deficits – came into being. The fashionable argument that the United States must not balance her accounts because in doing so she would deprive the world of much-needed international liquidity puts the cart before the horse. Big deficits of countries with a reserve currency create additional reserve *requirements* at the same time as creating additional reserves.

Even so, the adjustment of liquid reserves by the Board of Governors of the IMF may have its advantages, provided it is not done on an excessive scale. So long as SDRs constitute only a minor part of the total international liquid reserves the system might work reasonably satisfactorily. But once they become the principal element in monetary reserves the thought of a gathering of politicians deciding the amount of the bulk of liquid international reserves must give rise to gloomy forebodings. Admittedly it may have been bad enough when liquidity depended on the caprices of nature in the form of the discovery or non-discovery of new goldfields and the petering out of existing ones. It would prove to be a great deal worse if liquidity should depend on political compromises struck by representatives of a number of Governments, not according to the economic merits of the case but according to the balance of power amongst them and the degree of pressures to which each of them is subject.

Mr Barber was not clear, and indeed he could not be clear, about the rate at which, and the terms on which, existing reserve currencies would be converted into SDRs. All he said was that it would have to be done 'on a considerable scale', though gradually and over a period of time. Primarily he had in mind the problem of converting existing holdings of dollars into SDRs, but he also envisages the conversion of official sterling reserves of Sterling Area countries.

From the point of view of the possible inflationary character of this operation it may sound reassuring that any SDRs to be issued for the purpose of converting dollars or sterling would have to be matched by actual retirements of reserve currencies. But when he says 'retirement' he means transfer to the IMF, to a special account out of which SDRs might be issued, not if and when holders of sterling want to convert their holdings into SDRs, but when the IMF asks the reserve currency country to convert for another participant a particular balance of its currency. It would then draw SDRs from the special account of the IMF and the latter would hold the dollars or sterling. But I cannot imagine that the IMF would want to hold huge amounts of frozen dollars and sterling forever. They might be reissued through the General Drawing Accounts.

The basic idea that holders of dollar or sterling reserves, who would be quite content to continue to hold them, could be compelled to convert them into SDRs does not sound very attractive. It is true, it is one of the main rules of the original SDR scheme. But there is a difference between compelling surplus countries to convert moderate amounts of SDRs for deficit countries into currencies and compelling them to convert much larger amounts of old dollar or sterling reserves. Under the original SDR rules not only surplus countries can be instructed to convert SDRs but also deficit countries if, in the opinion of the IMF, they hold larger currency reserves than they need. If this should be true on a large scale under the new scheme it would be liable to induce some participants to withdraw from the scheme.

There is another aspect of this right of the IMF to compel unwilling participants to part with currency holdings which they might prefer to retain. There is no provision under the original rules to compel them to convert SDRs into gold. Assuming that this differentiation between currency reserves and gold reserves is retained in the new scheme, it would provide additional inducement for Central Banks to convert their currency reserves into gold. This cannot possibly be the intention of the authors of the scheme. But to empower the IMF to commandeer the participants' gold holdings might induce several countries to abstain from participating.

The whole scheme is based on the assumption that all or most participants would be willing to hold large amounts of SDRs in addition to their increased allocations. They would have to be willing to acquire from other participants twice the amount of their own original allocations, which would mean that they could be compelled to hold three times the amount of their allocations. Their holdings might reach considerable figures under the new scheme, more than they might want to hold, and they might prefer to withdraw from the scheme long before the limit is reached.

This brings us to the terms on which participants could

opt out. We saw in the last chapter that under the existing scheme these terms are very liberal indeed. A participant may cease to be a participant from the moment its letter notifying the IMF to that effect reaches the IMF. If it holds a larger amount of SDRs transferred to it than the amount it had transferred to other participants out of its allocation the IMF will repay it the difference at once and will then recoup the amounts spent by calling upon any of the remaining participants to accept and hold the amount involved. Should there be many important withdrawals the burden that is liable to arise from this provision – which appeared negligible under the original scheme – might well become unbearable and would lead to further withdrawals.

Conversely, should countries which have passed on to other participants more of their allocations than the amount they have converted for other participants withdraw, they are given a period of up to three years to restore the *status quo*. Again this delay may matter little so long as the outstanding total amounts to merely $9.5 billion. But if it is raised to many times the latter figure – which is the intention of the new plan – it might create a difficult situation.

It is no great exaggeration to say, therefore, that the new SDR system would be a fair-weather system. It would operate smoothly if conditions remained reasonably normal, but it is easy to visualise situations in which large-scale withdrawals would occur. Such an exodus would be self-aggravating. For, since the acceptability of SDRs depends on the degree of certainty of the recipient's ability to pass them on to other participants (there is no such thing as an international legal tender and SDRs are absolutely unsecured), the multiplication of their total and the removal of the little balance of payments discipline that exists under the original scheme is liable to reduce their acceptability quite considerably. The more participants deemed it in their interests to withdraw the less assurance the remaining participants would have that their SDRs would remain acceptable.

It is probably with this perturbing possibility in mind that so many people would like to see gold demonetised altogether. If there should be no preferable alternative to SDRs except discredited currencies participants are more likely to be willing to acquire and hold SDRs well in excess of their allocations. And we can trust theoreticians to create plausible theoretical foundations to even the most impracticable scheme. This task was performed by Machlup in the book quoted at the beginning of this chapter. He regards with pity mingled with contempt bankers and businessmen who still hold the old-fashioned view that money without intrinsic value of its own – or, for that matter, credit – should have some form of cover or should be subject to reserve requirements. The adoption of the original SDR scheme was, in his opinion, a real breakthrough. For their sole security lies in their acceptability, which is of course taken for granted. Yet under the original scheme participants who had parted with currencies against SDRs need not even repudiate their undertaking to get their money back, in certain well-defined conditions, and other participants must accept the re-converted SDRs if ordered to do so by the IMF. All they would have to do is contract out if they should be unwilling to accept and hold SDRs.

Conceivably, having regard to the intended big increase of the amount of SDRs, the authors of the definite scheme might deem it expedient to revise the original rules so that it might become more difficult to contract out and the terms on which it could be done might become less liberal. In that case acceptability depends on the extent to which participants feel bound by their solemn undertaking to the IMF. Is repudiation of the undertaking inconceivable? It would be easy, though hardly worth while, to compile a list of instances in which undertakings given to the IMF have been dishonoured, even by some of 'the best people'.

Nor is the much-emphasised gold guarantee of SDRs a safeguard that is liable to make SDRs very attractive to acquire and hold, except perhaps in exchange for some devaluation-prone currency. Monetary history can produce instances in which the guarantee given to the gold value of a currency was repudiated.

The best-known of these instances was the repudiation of the clause embodied in innumerable American loan contracts in the '30s, under which principal and interest on Government loans or on private borrowers' debts was payable in 'gold dollars of the present weight and fineness'. Following on this act of repudiation in 1933 a ban was placed in the United States and in a number of other countries on the conclusion of loan agreements containing a guarantee of the gold value of the liability. In any case, since SDRs are not a liability of the IMF or of any Central Bank or Government associated with it, it is difficult to imagine who could be called upon to implement the gold guarantee. Nobody could be held responsible even for the repayment of SDRs, let alone for the repayment of their full gold value.

To link SDRs with some composite monetary unit or with some index is open to doubts similar to the doubts raised by the gold guarantee. All such formulas would give rise to complications of accountancy and to legal complications whenever the value of the real currency in terms of SDR units changes.

In spite of all these objections, the idea of the British plan is most ingenious and its adoption might help us to get out of our present predicament. But it is essential to restrain the enthusiam with which it has been welcomed. It recalls the enthusiasm of John Law for his paper money scheme. John Law's paper money inspired confidence so long as its quantity was kept within reasonable limits. When it came to be inflated it became utterly discredited. This experience should be borne in mind by the authors of the SDR scheme.

I can well imagine how academic advocates of the SDR system would put all the blame for its failure on 'the politicians', just as John Law put the blame for the disastrous collapse of his system on the Regent and his extravagant Government. Our modern John Laws would not be able to plead ignorance of the deeply ingrained habits of politicians to misuse facilities placed at their disposal. It has occurred far too often since John Law's days.

The rules should be drafted so as to prevent the revised SDR scheme from becoming an inflationists' paradise. Of course I fully realise that in uttering such a warning note I have become guilty of what Machlup indicts as 'deliberate sabotage against world prosperity'. But I am fully prepared to face that indictment and my defence is that prosperity in the long run calls for slower growth and for consolidation of the growth achieved in recent decades. It was inflation that sabotaged prosperity in a great many countries.

Even in the absence of new allocations the SDR scheme is inherently expansionist, because while holders receive interest on their holdings those participants who have converted their holdings against currencies pay no interest on the amounts of currencies thus obtained. The expenses of the operation of the scheme are to be borne by the IMF. This means that year after year the outstanding total will be increased by the compound interest paid to holders in the form of further automatic allocations of SDRs. If the rate of interest is kept low this may not amount to very much in the short run. In order to make the device attractive the IMF would not even have to compete with interest rates obtainable by Central Banks if they held their reserves in the form of currencies. For it has the power to compel Central Banks to convert their currencies into SDRs.

Since it is the declared object of the scheme that in the course of time the bulk of monetary reserves should assume the form of SDRs, it may be safely taken for granted that the Board of Governors would be very generous with new allocations. This might well step up secular inflation. Even the proposed withdrawal of dollar and sterling reserves by converting them against SDRs is potentially inflationary beyond a certain stage. At present the world is saturated with excessive dollar and sterling reserves and this fact tends to limit the capacity of the United States and of Britain to contract more external short-term liabilities through an increase of non-resident holdings of dollars and sterling. But if foreign holdings of dollars or sterling are drastically reduced through the operation of the new SDR scheme this would open up the possibility for their increase. They would become much more confidence-inspiring through the consolidation of a substantial proportion of them, so that there would be much temptation and opportunity for allowing the foreign dollar and sterling balances to increase once more.

All this is pointed out not in order to condemn the scheme out of hand, but to explain that, should it be adopted, it would entail certain grave risks. We should accept those risks, but with our eyes wide open. This is important, because realisation of the pitfalls might induce the politicians and experts responsible for its elaboration to bear in mind the possibility of a failure of their scheme. A good general, even if he is certain to win the impending battle, does not neglect preparing plans for a retreat in case of a defeat.

To safeguard ourselves against a disastrous setback it would be expedient to proceed cautiously with the adoption of the new scheme and with the rate of its application. When we experiment with a new device or institution the inevitability of gradualness should be borne in mind. If the volume of Euro-dollars had jumped to $60 billion within a year or two from their initiation the result would have been in all probability a major crisis.

CHAPTER TWENTY-ONE

Is This the End of Bretton Woods?

IN the flood of comments that followed Mr Nixon's statement there was hardly any point on which a high proportion of commentators agreed. There was, however, one point on which there was virtual unanimity – that 15 August marked the end of the Bretton Woods system. As far as I know, the only dissenting voice was mine. I was firmly convinced that our return to the Bretton Woods system – subject to relatively major alterations – was only a question of time. Its restoration may take months or it may take years. But sooner or later the untidy situation created by the abandonment of stability would be tidied up. If by 'Bretton Woods' we mean the exact system laid down under the rules of the IMF, it may be correct to say that it will never return again. There are bound to be far-reaching changes. But to my mind 'Bretton Woods' stands for monetary stability. And I was firmly convinced that we would witness its return.

The main reason why the Bretton Woods system is so unpopular today is that those who had experience in the system of floating exchanges before the war have forgotten its disadvantages, while the memory of the disadvantages of rigid parities is still fresh in their minds. A high proportion of the present generation in Britain and in the United States never experienced floating exchanges. They are only familiar with the disadvantages of the undue rigidity with which the Bretton Woods system was applied on a number of occasions in most major countries, but they are quite unfamiliar with the much graver disadvantages of instability experienced by the last generation. In any case, most people seldom learn by experience gained in the past, or by experience gained in their time by other countries. Each generation in each country has to learn by its own experience and at its own cost. If, as seems possible, there should be henceforth prolonged periods of floating exchanges, there will be ample opportunity for economists, politicians and administrators to familiarise themselves with the disadvantages of the system of their choice.

In that case, bankers, businessmen and the general public would have ample opportunity to discover at their cost the difference between stability and instability. Before the war those affected directly by erratic exchanges constituted an insignificant percentage of Britons and of Americans. When British people were told after the suspension of the gold standard in September 1931 that the pound would remain a pound it was technically true as far as well over 90 per cent of the population was concerned. There was considerably less justification for Mr Wilson's promise in 1967 that the devaluation of sterling would not affect the pound in our pocket. For in the meantime the number of those directly or indirectly interested in exchange movements has increased very considerably. Which fact did not prevent Mr Nixon from borrowing Mr Wilson's discredited formula in his announcement of 15 August, without acknowledging his source.

Quite apart from the increase in the volume of foreign trade and the number of firms and their employees directly interested in it, there was a sharp increase during the past decade or two in the number of people in every country who acquired the habit of spending their holidays abroad. Many of them have already had some unpleasant experience as a result of the adoption of floating exchanges. Apart from the possibility of a depreciation of the money they want to spend abroad, under floating exchanges they are exposed to exploitation by banks and travel agancies who take full advantage of the fluctuations of exchange rates by charging or allowing distinctly unfavourable exchange rates to those wanting to buy foreign notes or to sell travellers' cheques. So long as the fluctuations remain narrow the irritation caused by such exploitation is a minor nuisance. When fluctuations widen the actual losses suffered by the tourists might cause serious inconvenience. Millions of tourists will then have good cause to curse the system which has deprived them of the near-certainty they enjoyed most of the time under the system of stability. As they are a vocal section of the community their protests are certain to get wide publicity.

Those engaged in foreign trade will have much more reason for being dissatisfied with the system of floating exchanges. The uncertainty of exchange rates will induce a great many of them who seldom covered their exchange risks under stable exchanges to do so regularly under floating exchanges. The increase in the demand for forward exchange facilities will be accompanied by a decline in the amount of such facilities available. Because of the increased degree of uncertainty and the possibility of bigger losses through wider fluctuations, banks are likely to reduce their maximum limits to which they will be prepared to deal in forward exchanges either in the market or with their customers. Or they will increase the cost of the forward exchange facilities to a level at which it will cease to be profitable to transact business in goods on which the profit margin is narrow.

No doubt Governments will be pressed to provide adequate forward exchange facilities for genuine commercial require-ments at a reasonable cost. As already pointed out earlier, judging by the British experience during the period of exchange control, this would be very expensive for Governments, because of the one-sided use importers and exporters would make of the facilities. They would only avail themselves of the facilities offered when it suits their interests.

As a result of unfavourable experience with floating ex-changes by business firms and by tourists, the number of those who will grow tired of floating exchanges is likely to increase. What is more important, the general public will discover in due course that under the system the dice are loaded against the consumer. They will find that whenever the national currency depreciates importers and retailers will lose no time in adjusting their prices to the higher costs of goods in terms of national currency. But an appreciation of the national currency will not be followed by a downward adjustment of the prices of imported goods, or at any rate it will only be followed after a time lag and not to anything like to the full extent.

Once this comes to be widely realised there will be growing pressure of public opinion in favour of returning to stability. Economists and others who have been advocating floating exchanges will find that the number of their enthusiastic supporters will dwindle.

Central Banks and Treasuries will discover in due course that it is, in given circumstances, even more difficult to defend a floating rate against an unwanted degree of appreciation than it had been to defend fixed rates against devaluation or revaluation. They will need at least as strong reserves and at least as heavy foreign support as under the Bretton Woods system, and they will find that it might become much more difficult, amidst the atmosphere created by a currency war, to supplement their reserves by foreign credits. In any case Central Banks will become reluctant to part with their surpluses, since the trend might well turn against their currencies after an excessive appreciation due to the self-aggravating character of exchange movements under the system of floating exchanges. There will be much less international co-operation. It will be a case of 'everybody for himself'. Although in a given situation some Governments or Central Banks may feel it to be in accordance with their interest to make arrangements for unilateral or reciprocal assistance, there will be little left of the systematic assistance that became a matter of routine during the long period of international stability amidst the Bretton Woods spirit of co-operation.

Governments will find it difficult to plan their policies owing to the uncertainty of the trend of their exchanges. While occasionally their Central Banks might intervene successfully in the market of floating exchanges, sooner or later they are likely to be caught. And in a competitive currency depreciation or appreciation race there can in the long run be no winners, only losers. Those responsible for the shaping of foreign exchange policy, monetary policy and economic policy will be longing sooner or later to return to the security of stable conditions.

As both the United States and Britain had suffered heavy losses through the prolonged defence of their currencies at an overvalued level they are understandably less keen on stability than Germans or Frenchmen. But even their Governments and public opinions are liable to discover sooner or later that the disadvantages of undue flexibility are apt to be much graver than those of undue rigidity.

The experiment in floating exchanges during August–December 1971 provided no real test for the much-advocated system of floating exchanges. Its supporters, having expected that floating exchanges had come to stay, were naturally disappointed by the early restabilisation of all principal currencies after only four months of floating. They now seek comfort from the fact that the suspension of stability did not result in any major crisis. But, as was pointed out in the last chapter, this was because of the absence of any acute political or economic crisis. Any system can operate reasonably well during such a calm period.

Should the authorities feel impelled to intervene in the market on their own initiative they are liable to incur grave risks. It is true during recent years they suffered staggering losses on such intervention when parities were changed or suspended. The outstanding instances for such losses are the losses suffered by the British Exchange Equalisation Account on the devaluation of sterling in 1967 and the losses suffered by the German and Japanese authorities on the revaluation of their own currencies in 1971. Such losses are liable to occur more frequently under fluctuating exchanges.

When Mr Nixon announced the suspension of the convertibility of the dollar and the adoption of the floating dollar was followed by the adoption of floating exchanges by most of the leading countries the advocates of the system of floating exchanges were triumphant. Their belief that the new system had come to stay was encouraged by spokesmen of a number of Governments who all paid lip-service to the advantages of floating exchanges. But in retrospect it seems doubtful if many of them really regarded the floating of their exchanges, or those of other countries, as more than a temporary device to ascertain the whereabouts of the equilibrium rates at which their exchanges would be re-stabilised in due course.

It seems probable that some Governments pretended to favour floating exchanges largely in order to strengthen their bargaining position, especially in relation to the French Government, a staunch defender of stability. Since throughout the '60s and early '70s France was very difficult to negotiate with and was in the habit of vetoing any agreement unless the French terms were accepted it was hoped that, owing to her keenness on returning to stability, she would be willing to make concessions for the sake of overcoming the opposition of other countries to an early stabilisation.

During the course of the autumn the number of Governments keen on re-stabilising after an agreed realignment of parities and a broadening of the band between supportpoint increased. None of them was prepared, however, to revalue their currencies as part of an all-round realignment without the participation of the United States in the realignment through a moderate devaluation of the dollar.

For a long time the idea was firmly resisted by the United States, though after the September meeting of the IMF Mr Nixon and Mr Connally were less stubborn. They drifted into the habit of blowing hot and cold. Indeed Mr Connally surprised the Rome Conference in November 1971 by foreshadowing the possibility of a devaluation of the dollar by up to 10 per cent. Thereafter, however, his pronouncements were alternating between categorical rejection of the idea of raising the price of gold and hints of the possibility of such decision.

It looked for some time as if the fate of the dollar depended on whether the final decision would be taken on an even day when the administration was willing to consider a devaluation or on an odd day when that solution was emphatically rejected.

The sudden change of Mr Nixon's attitude at his meeting with M. Pompidou and the ensuing acceptance of a detailed realignment formula at the Washington meeting of the Group of Ten Finance Ministers might well be described as an

'American Miracle'. For even though the United States succeeded in achieving the revaluation of most currencies, and the
band came to be widened, she agreed to an immediate removal
of the protectionist measures without immediate *quid pro quo*
and she did not insist on a definite commitment about a long-
term currency reform. The elaboration of an extension of the
SDR system on the lines suggested by Mr Barber was left for
future negotiations. Yet it was important from an American
point of view to obtain without much delay large allocations of
SDRs for the purpose of 'consolidating' the excessive dollar
reserves held by Central Banks and meeting the apparently
intractable balance of payments deficit.

The sudden change of the American policy from obstructive
pig-headedness to an incomparably more conciliatory attitude
was as surprising as it was inexplicable. We had the choice
between a number of possible alternative explanations; each of
them, or any combination of them, might have been responsible for Mr Nixon's increased willingness to collaborate in the
effort to find a solution instead of trying to dictate its terms.
The following is a selection of them:

(1) As already mentioned above, possibly the declared preference for floating was only meant to serve as a bargaining
weapon, and the appreciation of most other currencies in terms
of dollars obviated the necessity for its further use.

(2) Mr Nixon and his advisers came to realise the gravity
of the disadvantages and risks attached to prolonged instability and of the risk of an aggravation of conditions as a
result of some political or economic crisis.

(3) The possibility of a trade war or currency war with other
countries of the free world as a result of their retaliation to
American measures had to be taken into consideration. Such
developments might have split the free world into two hostile
camps and would have weakened Mr Nixon's bargaining position on the occasion of his impending visit to Peking and
Moscow.

(4) Mr Nixon came to realise that the United States had
ceased to be financial dictator of the free world and that the

monetary balance of power had changed to a considerable extent in favour of countries of Western Europe and of Japan. As a result he had to deal with them on a more or less equal footing.

(5) Owing to the urgency of the adoption of some reform more or less on the lines of the Barber Plan it was essential to remove the main obstacle to it by finding a solution for the immediate problem.

(6) The extent to which uncertainty and instability was actually beginning to handicap foreign trade and investment came to be realised in Washington. The possibility of a slump as a result of the paralysing effect of prolonged uncertainty must have gone a long way towards inducing Mr Nixon to come to terms, especially as unemployment in the United States called for urgent remedies.

(7) Possibly Mr Nixon and his advisers came to realise the gross inconsistency of advocating the demonetisation of gold while making heavy sacrifices and taking heavy risks for the sake of avoiding a change in the meaningless official gold parity.

(8) Finally the untidy situation created by the instability of the dollar and of other currencies, and its unfavourable effect on American business conditions, and an unfavourable effect on Mr Nixon's prospect at the November Presidential election.

For some or all of these reasons, Mr Nixon lifted his veto to an early re-stabilisation. At the same time, official spokesmen stressed that the new parities would be looked upon as being less firmly established than the Bretton Woods parities had been, so that if it should be found that their maintenance would encounter difficulties they would not be defended as stubbornly as the Bretton Woods parities had been. Moreover, since the dollar was not to occupy such a central position as in the Bretton Woods system and parities would be expressed in gold or in SDR units there would be less reason for considering the dollar as immutable, so that the United States would consider herself in the same position as any other country in respect of her freedom to change her parities.

It seems unlikely but not impossible that the world could

ever return to the Bretton Woods system in the exact form in which it operated from 1946 till 1971. It is true, the dollar is no longer qualified for serving as the basic currency on which the system could be rebuilt. It has become too much weakened and discredited to be suitable for its old role – but a drastic devaluation would restore its strength at its lower parity. At the time of writing this appears most unlikely, as this solution is anathema to Mr Nixon and Mr Connally. But politicians are apt to change their attitude, and countries are apt to change the politicians – as they did in 1932 – if they come to disapprove of their policies. It is also possible that Mr Nixon or his successor might be forced into major devaluation as a result of a sweeping flight to gold causing a spectacular rise in the market price of gold. This would create a *fait accompli* which Congress and Administration might accept.

But even in the absence of a major devaluation of the dollar the Bretton Woods system need not be a matter of the past as its opponents hope it to become. In fact, under the formula adopted on 18 December 1971 the international monetary system has reverted to the Bretton Woods system to the extent of at least 75 per cent. Once more there are gold parities and official support points, even if the spread between them is wider. Most Governments are expected to endeavour to maintain their exchanges within these support points. Even if it is the declared intention of the United States Government and of other Governments not to defend the parities as stubbornly as they were defended during the past quarter century, this attitude does not conflict with the letter and spirit of the Bretton Woods system, under which fundamental disequilibrium justified changes of parities. The undue rigidity with which parities were defended in many instances was contrary to the Bretton Woods spirit, so that the adoption of a more flexible attitude will mean a return to the Bretton Woods system as envisaged by its authors and not a departure from it.

CHAPTER TWENTY-TWO

We Must Have a Reserve Currency

FEARS of inflation through a too rapid expansion of the volume of SDRs are of course a matter for controversy, and one's attitude depends on one's general attitude towards expansion. But an unduly rapid expansion of SDRs could be opposed also on less controversial grounds. The extent of Central Banks' requirements of conventional currency reserves for the purpose of intervention seems to have been played down by Mr Barber. He readily conceded that, since transactions in SDRs would remain confined to the public sector and the private sector would continue to deal in conventional foreign exchanges, Central Banks would have to keep 'working balances' in the form of foreign currencies for their requirements for official intervention in the market. But if he and his advisers envisage the prospects of official balances in foreign currencies being ever reduced to the equivalents of petty cash holdings of business firms they will have to think again.

It is true, if the new system should work as its authors expect it to work it might reduce large-scale buying and selling pressures on undervalued or overvalued exchanges. But it would not eliminate such pressures. For its adoption would not provide the authorities with some magic formula enabling them to ascertain whether current exchange rates are in accordance with their equilibrium levels. Being human they are liable to miscalculate the whereabouts of that level, or they might pretend not to realise that their currency is overvalued, in order to avoid having to take awkward measures at an inconvenient moment to restore equilibrium.

In any case, speculators, importers and exporters and investors might take from time to time – rightly or wrongly – the view that one exchange is depreciation-prone and another appreciation-prone. They act on their beliefs in their operations. It is true, it would be easier for the authorities to meet the resulting supply–demand imbalance in the market by converting SDRs which would be at their disposal, and the use of which would not have to be preceded by difficult negotiations in Basle or Washington. But the ease with which they could meet a deficiency of supply in foreign exchanges would merely defer the necessity for taking steps to correct the disequilibrium that is the cause of the pressure in the market. In the absence of corrective measures, sooner or later the imbalance might assume such dimensions that it would necessitate the use of very large amounts of SDRs. A stage might be reached at which surplus countries would have reached the statutory limits of their holdings of SDRs and would refuse to convert more than that limit – twice their own allocation. In that situation the country concerned would have to resort to the much-deferred devaluation or deflation, neither of which would have been made easier by the delay.

Devaluations might be deferred without basic justification by official intervention to support the national currency with the aid of the SDR holdings of the Central Bank concerned. For the purpose of such intervention on a large scale – which is a frequently present possibility – Central Banks would have to keep substantial amounts of 'working capital' in the form of conventional foreign exchange reserves.

In any case, there would be a long period of transition during which Central Banks would have to continue to keep foreign exchanges well in excess of the amount covering their immediate or foreseeable requirements of 'working capital'.

It is bound to take time before the plan is finalised, even though the negotiators could ill afford to take anything like five years over it, as their forerunners did over the original SDR plan. Although the new plan is infinitely more important, so that it is vital to avoid taking the wrong line, its adoption is now a matter of great urgency. Even so, it cannot be rushed through.

What is likely to happen is that a second issue of SDRs

based on the original scheme on the terms agreed upon in 1967 might be allocated, pending the conclusion of an agreement over the major plan. Although the SDRs may be allocated on the original terms, Mr Barber foreshadowed the adoption of the revised terms with retrospective effect to cover the SDRs already allocated and even transferred to other participants. But even after such an increase of Central Banks holdings of SDRs they would still continue to represent a small proportion of their total monetary reserves. It would take a number of years before they came to represent the major part of the reserves, and even then the proportion would vary from Central Bank to Central Bank.

In the meantime the world will continue to need an international reserve currency. Sterling might also retain its limited role as a reserve currency for the Sterling Area countries – at any rate until Britain's integration with the EEC would end that role. In any event the process of diversification of Sterling Area countries' reserves is likely to make further progress, accelerated by the deliberate policy towards diversification foreshadowed in Mr Barber's statement.

After the adoption of the plan there would be a transition period in the course of which the SDRs to be created would be gradually allocated. Pending their full allocation Central Banks would have to continue to hold large amounts of currencies in their reserves. I am convinced that if it depended on certain Central Banks they would prefer to hold permanently a high percentage of their reserves in the form of gold and currencies. Under Mr Barber's proposals the IMF would have power to compel Central Banks to convert their holdings of currencies into SDRs, and if Mr Connally should have his way the IMF would be able to commandeer also their gold reserves. But I doubt if large holders of gold would ever consent to this. Rather than convert their gold for 'paper gold' they would stay out of the scheme, or they would join it and withdraw as soon as the IMF tried to use this power to any substantial extent.

We saw in the last chapter that even after the complete adoption of the plan Central Banks would have to hold 'working capital' in the form of currencies for the purpose of intervening in the foreign exchange market. It is a highly controversial question whether currency requirements would remain high even after the adoption of the scheme. To a large degree the Special Drawing Account of the IMF would play the part of an international clearing house. It would play the part which the BIS was originally meant to play. Holdings derived from surplus purchases of foreign exchanges by some Central Banks would be offset by requirements arising to other Central Banks from surplus sales of foreign currencies in support of their national currencies. To some extent this clearing might divert official operations from the open market. But in spite of this clearing the volume of private transactions would remain large.

One is permitted to wonder if there had been much less speculation, less capital movements and less leading and lagging if the SDR system had been in existence during recent years. On the one hand, automatic access of Central Banks to support as a matter of daily routine instead of having to negotiate it once in six months or twelve months might have discouraged speculative operations based on anticipation of devaluations or revaluations. On the other hand the knowledge that parities would not have been defended with such determination as they were during the operation of the Bretton Woods system would have encouraged such operations. What the net effect of these conflicting currents would have been on the extent of the pressures – and, what is much more important, what the net effect would be after the adoption of the proposed SDR reform – is of course anybody's guess. Even a successful defence of parities with the aid of the increased allocations of SDRs might lead to large-scale pressures, because the difference between the degrees of inflations or deflations in various countries would affect the size of their trade surpluses or deficits.

It would be sheer wishful thinking, therefore, to assume that thanks to the operation of the SDR scheme the volume of official transactions in the markets would necessarily become moderate even in the long run, apart altogether from the more or less prolonged transition period that must necessarily precede the full application of the plan. Since the turnover is likely to be very large from time to time, the Central Banks would have to be prepared to cope with it when necessary. Although they would be in a position to replenish their reserves of foreign currencies with the aid of their holdings of SDRs, they might find it expedient to be able to intervene without even a minimum of delay involved in the operation of the somewhat cumbersome mechanism of the device. The currency reserves would be their first line of defence and their SDRs their second line of defence.

No matter how substantial the amounts of SDRs allocated to Central Banks, their holdings might not necessarily be sufficient in all conceivable circumstances to meet their requirements in case of particularly heavy or prolonged pressure. It should not therefore be taken for granted that under the new system surpluses and deficiencies would always necessarily clear each other automatically. Which is just as well. For if Governments were able to assume that, once the system has become fully operative, they would live happily ever after even if it were to deprive them of the incentive to pursue sound policies the cost of their optimism might be very heavy in the long run. If they realise the possibilities of a breakdown of the system they might find it expedient to possess, in addition to their SDRs, some reserve currency assets rather than depend on being always able to have their SDRs converted into currencies. Indeed the possession of strong currencies which would be freely acceptable for meeting deficits might be considered somewhat safer than the possession of SDRs, though not so safe as the holding of gold.

From the above observations it is obvious that even after the adoption and full implementation of the SDR scheme, and even if the resulting SDR allocations are fairly frequent, there is definitely a need also for a reserve currency or several reserve currencies. Another reason why this is essential is that there must be some device to fall back upon without delay if for any reason the SDR system should break down. Its collapse must not be allowed to leave a monetary power-vacuum behind in the middle of the crisis which caused its collapse.

Of course gold would meet fully the requirements as an alternative to SDRs if they should become discredited as a result of overissue, or for no matter what other reason. Unfortunately there would not be enough monetary gold available to take the place of the inflated volume of SDRs. Hence the need for a reserve currency which would remain in use while SDRs are the principal reserve asset and which would then be able to resume their former role as the main reserve asset.

Should the United States make full use of the respite from pressure on the dollar for restoring confidence in it the dollar would be the obvious currency for that role. Although the situation is liable to change, there is no reason to believe that the American economy would not remain the strongest economy. Pursuit of a sound policy would restore the prestige of the dollar and the financial power of the United States. A collapse of the SDR system would be almost certain to be accompanied by escalated inflation, in which case a drastic devaluation of the dollar and of all other currencies would have to precede the restoration of normal conditions. Otherwise there might not be sufficient monetary gold to take the place of the liquidity represented by SDRs.

To qualify for resuming its former role, the dollar would have to be backed by a substantial gold reserve reinforced by means of disinvestment advocated in Chapter 11 and by the achievement of a satisfactory balance of payments over a period of years. This latter would necessitate some degree of self-discipline in the sphere of domestic consumption and the recovery of the American character which, like the British, became debased during the '60s and early '70s. What is needed more than anything else in the United States as in Britain is national regeneration and a return of the spirit which had made both Anglo-Saxon countries great.

It is conceivable that the dollar would encounter competition for the role of reserve currency. Possibly by then sterling will have given up altogether that role as a result of the termination or disintegration of the Sterling Area. Possibly some form of European monetary unit might develop in the course of time, though it must be preceded by advanced economic and political integration of the enlarged Common Market. It might be beneficial for the dollar and for the United States if the European monetary unit were to compete with the dollar for leadership, for one of the reasons why the American balance of payments and the dollar were allowed to deteriorate in the '6os was the deterioration of sterling, which had been principal rival to the dollar.

The technical facilities provided by the New York money market have improved beyond recognition and are likely to improve further. But Americans should learn from the British experience that the excellence of such facilities, though helpful, is no substitute for a sound economy and that it is not sufficient to ensure the supremacy of the dollar either as a reserve asset supplementing SDRs or as a reserve currency to take the place of SDRs if the proposed experiment with the latter should fail.

Even if the experiment with the SDR system should not fail there would be ample justification for the maintenance of a reserve currency, or possibly several reserve currencies. To rely exclusively on SDRs for meeting all requirements of the international monetary system would be like relying exclusively on the United Nations for our national security. It would be as ill-advised to neglect ensuring the existence of at least one reserve currency as it would be to neglect our national defences on the assumption that the United Nations would safeguard us from enemy aggression.

CHAPTER TWENTY-THREE

Could the Dollar Regain Supremacy?

THE fact that it was the British Governor of the IMF who took the initiative for the adoption of SDRs as the international reserve currency implied a final gesture completing sterling's abdication from that role. It seems possible and even probable, however, that Britain sponsored the SDR system in full agreement with the United States, reached prior to Mr Barber's announcement. Presumably the reason why it was not Mr Connally who proposed the reform was that the United States was still too dollar-proud to bring herself to performing such an act of abdication in the blaze of international publicity. Even though various recent American official pronouncements indicate that the Nixon Administration is fully alive to the disadvantages and risks involved in possessing the leading international currency, it is not likely to remain the official policy to abandon that role of the dollar altogether and forever.

For one thing, it would be bound to take a long time before the SDR scheme could become fully operative and during the period of transition the world would need the dollar for performing the various tasks of an international currency. And, as I tried to show in the last chapter, even after the full adoption of the SDR plan, foreign currencies would retain a more important role than is envisaged in Mr Barber's scheme. The dollar would then stand by far the best chance to play the leading role among these currencies.

In spite of the suspension of its convertibility and the subsequent official policy of its depreciation and its mini-devaluation, the dollar retained much of the important part it played before Mr Nixon's announcement. Central Banks could not help continuing to use it as their principal, if not only, reserve and intervention currency. Since all currencies had become undependable and international business had to be transacted in terms of foreign currencies, a high proportion of it continued to be transacted in dollars even during the months of its downward floating.

The dollar continued to be used as the main currency for short-term financing, largely owing to the incontestable supremacy of the Euro-dollar market over other Euro-currency markets. Possibly a gradual conversion of dollar reserves into SDRs in the course of time might siphon many billions of dollars out of the market. But judging by past experience, whenever something happened which tended to reduce the importance of the Euro-dollar market, something else also happened which increased its turnover to new record levels. There appears to be no reason to believe that it would be otherwise this time. In any case, it is bound to take quite a number of years before the process of converting dollar surpluses into SDRs will be completed – if indeed it will ever be completed.

The dollar's international role as the currency of the Euro-issue market is not quite so well assured. For years the Deutsche-mark played an important part as a currency of Euro-issues, and both Euro-bonds and Euro-equities have also been issued in terms of other currencies and of composite monetary units. But in this sphere too the dollar recovered in 1971 its lead even before it became stabilised.

International trade continues to be invoiced to a large extent in dollars, even though more importers and exporters now insist on having their goods invoiced in some other currency. Once confidence in the stability of the dollar at its new parities is restored, prices in international trade will be quoted and invoiced once more in terms of dollars to the same extent as before 15 August 1971.

Foreign exchange business in foreign exchange markets is still transacted on the basis of dollar cross rates of other currencies and the dollar continues to be the most important foreign exchange in London. But whether it will retain its leading position in the above spheres depends on the willingness and ability of the United States to pursue sound policies. This cannot be taken for granted, for, although the dollar is no longer floating, there will continue to be much temptation and much opportunity for the United States Government to pursue the unsound policies to which the dollar owes the cessation of its supremacy.

No doubt the United States has retained the economic superiority which is a preliminary condition for the recovery of the dollar's prestige. But economic superiority is not in itself sufficient. After all, it was not able to save the dollar from the decline of its prestige. It would have been necessary to combine economic strength with a degree of self-restraint in keeping down domestic consumption for the sake of maintaining adequate balance of payments surpluses, or at any rate avoiding gigantic balance of payments deficits. It would also have been necessary to resist the temptation to invest too much abroad, not only because it affected the capital side of the balance of payments immediately, but also because it increased the relative strength of the economies of other countries and assisted them in competing for markets – domestic as well as foreign – for American goods produced in the United States.

Having regard to the excess of American short-term liabilities over the American gold stock, it would take a prolonged effort to restore the basic strength of the dollar. Even if under the Barber Plan the United States were to be gradually relieved of the bulk of her external short-term liabilities the resulting liability in SDRs would have to be paid off to restore the self-respect of the American people. In the absence of a consolidating operation the dollar would remain under a cloud. Its relative strength might increase through revaluations of other currencies. But in order to increase its absolute basic strength the American people would have to make a prolonged supreme effort to achieve an 'American miracle' comparable with the 'German miracle', the 'Japanese miracle' and the 'Italian miracle'.

It might take a major crisis – an economic 'Pearl Harbour' – to induce the American nation to abandon or mitigate its wasteful consuming habits by which perfectly serviceable goods are discarded as soon as new models are introduced, because their possession is a supreme status symbol. And the strike weapon is resorted to far too often and on far too large a scale to make it easy for the United States to live up to her old reputation for efficiency and productivity. Unless the American nation makes a supreme effort to regain its old virtues the dollar's chances of maintaining its supremacy in the long run cannot be assessed very high. Unless the dollar becomes once more a symbol of sound finance there would be a possibility that some other currency might capture the lead. Germany or some other country might develop an ambition to that end. Both Germany and Japan possess strong economies and if they deemed it worth thier while to achieve a leading position for their respective currencies either of them would stand a good chance of replacing the dollar unless the United States recovers her economic dynamism. Even a 'British miracle' that might restore sterling to its traditional position – subject to the limitations imposed on it by the SDR scheme and by integration into the EEC—is possible if unlikely. I cannot assess the chances of a combined European currency very high as a rival to the dollar.

From the point of view of power politics it would be infinitely preferable if the United States were to recover her supremacy in the monetary sphere, because of the power and prestige attached to that supremacy. It is essential to enable America to continue to play the part of the principal defender of the free world. From this point of view Mr Heath's remarks at the Conservative Party Conference on 16 October 1971, that the United States could no longer be relied upon for assistance, expressed excessive defeatism – presumably for the purpose of trying to strengthen the case for Britain joining the Common Market.

The short cut towards achieving supremacy for the dollar amidst the changed conditions to be brought about by the proposed reform would be of course a drastic devaluation of the dollar and the restoration of its convertibility. The dollar's prestige was based on the knowledge that it represented a fixed quantity of gold. It is true, private individuals or business firms, whether residents or non-residents, were not entitled to convert their dollars into gold. But the knowledge that the United States authorities were able and willing to convert official dollar holdings into gold was sufficient to identify the dollar with gold. The dollar's prestige could be restored even if the quantity of gold to which it is equated should be fixed much below its old parity.

It cannot be restated sufficiently often or with sufficient emphasis that the prestige of a currency depends not on its past record but on its present position and its future prospects. The repeated devaluations of Latin American currencies do not restore their prestige because, even though they might be dependable for the moment at their devalued levels, another devaluation in the not too distant future is usually well within the realm of possibility. But considering that the previous devaluation of the dollar was in 1934 it is reasonable to assume that if it were devalued substantially the exercise would not recur for a long time to come. In order that the dollar should inspire that degree of confidence a mini-devaluation might not be sufficient. After devaluation by a mere 8 per cent, or by even more, it might be widely assumed that another instalment would follow before very long. Indeed, a small devaluation is less confidence-inspiring than the rigid maintenance of the parity at an over-valued level. For once the principle that the parity is subject to changes is conceded, the possibility, indeed the probability, of another devaluation comes to be readily assumed.

The realignment of parities in 1971 removed one objection to devaluation – that if all currencies were devalued to the same extent the dollar would remain overvalued and at its new parities and would become just as much subject to adverse pressure through an adverse balance of payments as it had been prior to its devaluation.

The establishment of parities in terms of SDRs instead of gold would remove another objection to devaluation. This aspect of the plan was brought out clearly by Mr Barber on 28 September, even though he was obviously not thinking in terms of a drastic devaluation. Nor would the resulting increase of the book-keeping value of gold reserves conflict with the application and successful operation of the SDR scheme. Quite on the contrary, it would mitigate the pressure for excessive allocations of SDRs and would give the system a chance to establish itself on sound foundations through its gradual application.

There is no reason why the use of revalued gold for reserves should not be reconciled with the adoption of SDRs for the same purpose. The proposed reform would enable Central Banks to make less use of the gold exchange standard. Any inadequacy of the gold reserves could be corrected through allocations of SDRs. The existence of a large monetary gold stock in the background would inspire confidence in the new system and this would go a long way towards ensuring its successful operation. The answer to the world's problem lies in a restoration of the dollar's lead among currencies and the combination of convertible currencies, SDRs and gold as reserve currencies.

The rehabilitation of the dollar and the writing up of the book-keeping value of gold would come useful if the SDR scheme should fail as a result of its misuse. That possibility must not be ignored, and the existence of a system to fall back upon if necessary might save us from a major disaster that might arise if we should rely exclusively on the SDR system.

For this reason, but even more for political reasons which transcend economic considerations, the destiny of the free world is closely linked with the destiny of the dollar. Our hope to survive as free nations depends to a very high degree on the restoration of the financial and political power of the United States through the restoration of the dollar's strength. It would be a fatal mistake if unduly generous allocation of SDRs should encourage American official opinion and public opinion in their present deplorable inclination to seek to achieve their ends in the easy way instead of endeavouring to achieve them in the hard but lasting way. It would be fatal if America followed Britain's bad example in taking the line of least resistance by relinquishing her ambition to restore her currency to its proper position in the international monetary system.

In a sense the United States appears to have succeeded in making a halt on the slippery slope. In December 1971 the irresponsible experiment of the floating dollar was brought to an end, even though Mr Nixon did not muster up enough courage to solve the dollar's problem by a sufficiently drastic devaluation to place it entirely above suspicion. We shall probably go through a period during which the viability of the devalued dollar will be sought to be tested through trial and error. Quite conceivable its mini-devaluation might not prove to have been sufficient to ensure the restoration of its full prestige and power.

However this may be, it would be essential for the American authorities to show that they themselves have full confidence in the devalued dollar. This they could only show convincingly if they made it their declared official ambition to restore the dollar to its old role as the principal reserve currency. Display of undue dependence on SDRs would show a lack of courage and confidence, and a lack of determination to pursue policies which would reassure the world about the destiny of the dollar.

Above all, it would be essential to make a supreme effort to check the inflationary trend in the United States by balancing the budget and by giving up, for the time being, the policy of cheap money which inspires distrust in the dollar at its new level. The dollar cannot be trusted until the equilibrium of the balance of payments is restored.

Index